Days of Glory: Down Pine Island Sound when the waters were smooth as glass and reflected shadows came the exciting floating palaces of the "railroad kings," bringing mail, cargo, and occasional passengers to the offshore "bulkheads"— later to the wharves of the islands. But history began long, long before . . . —Photo courtesy the Eleanor Pearse estate

The Unknown Story of
Sanibel and Captiva
(Ybel y Cautivo)

By Florence Fritz
1901-1969

Standard Book Number 87012-165-0
Library of Congress Card Number 73-93790
Printed in the United States of America
Copyright ©1974 by Lelia Morris Cunningham
Fort Myers, Florida, U.S.A.

First Printing 1974
Second Printing 1975

Printed by McClain Printing Company
Parsons, West Virginia, U.S.A.
1974

Books by Florence Fritz

Try Florida Ways for Happier Days

*Bamboo & Sailing Ships: the story
    of Thomas A. Edison in Fort Myers*

Unknown Florida

*The Unknown Story of Sanibel and Captiva
                    (Ybel   y   Cautivo)*

Preface

This book is the story of two islands—Sanibel and Captiva—and what happened to them and their people.

The account was begun to tell the story of the homesteaders and the happy days of their past which those who had lived then and their descendants could never forget.

One thing led to another and it became necessary to write Part I to tell what went before and then Part III had to be included to explain what happened after the homesteaders were gone.

It seemed necessary to use some footnotes for the benefit of future historians but these have been placed in the Appendix where they can be properly consulted by those who desire them and not interfere with the pleasure of those who do not need them. A Bibliography has been added for the same reason.

The book is primarily a record of homesteaders and their descendants, of their times and ways, when the United States was in the days of its youth, and people found freedom if they wished for it on these islands by the sea. Yet the three parts together add dimensions that should make the story of interest to all people.

Throughout the pages the words Light House (or L.H. or L.H.B.) have been used instead of lighthouse and capitalized to emphasize the importance of it and their service to mariners and early settlers long before men took to land ways and the skies.

Caloosahatchee has been written as two words for a similar reason plus another. *Hatchee,* in Seminole, means "river." When the Seminoles were fleeing southward in Florida before advancing American soldiers long ago, they came at last into the Caloosa Nation's territory in southern Florida. The

Seminoles called the river after the original inhabitants: the Caloosa *Hatchee* or Caloosa River, for it had been the main water highway of those people, connecting its cities, villages, and provinces that even then were almost gone.

In these pages, during the years from 1876 on, the upriver village is sometimes referred to as *Myers,* other times as *Fort* Myers. The reason is that the United States Post Office Department objected to having two Fort Myers in the American nation and there was already one called Fort Myer in Virginia. For twenty-five years arguments seesawed between the village and Washington. In 1901 local persistence triumphed. Fort Myers, Florida, became the official name of the village which meanwhile had become the county seat of Lee County from whence came decisions regarding the early schools of the islands.

In early chapters words like *smoak, cavear, papayers,* etc., appear. They are contained in writings of early adventurers who were not always particular as to how a word was spelled or consistent in their unusual methods of spelling. Yet they add a flavor of those times and seemed worthy of note for that reason.

Acknowledgments

In the beginning, it is fitting that acknowledgments be made as to the primary sources of information for the story of Sanibel and Captiva as well as to the many whose efforts have made the compilation possible.

Interviewing people and gathering photographs began more than three decades ago. Recently, additional interviews were made with those who were still living. From these came experiences, memories, and events that no printed source will throw light on.

Many a man or woman could give only a disconnected part of a fact; and often in the process of composition these have been welded, without naming the source, one fragment into another.

The names that appear next almost surely represent less than a majority of the individuals who have at some time or another contributed some fragment to this story. An asterisk (*) indicates that the person named is no longer living.

Mrs. Annie Allred, Scotia Bryant, Francis Bailey, G. W. Bryant,* Monroe "Buddy" Bobst and Elizabeth Bobst, Jesse and Bessie Gibson Carter, Captain R. C. and Lillias Cockerill,** Eleanor Clapp, Jack* and Gertrude Cole, Captain Leon and Mrs. Crumpler, Rosamond Lee Chadwick,* Enid Cockerill Donohue, Captain J. J. Dinkins,* Rev. George W. Gatewood,* Hattie Brainard Gore,* Arthur Gibson, Leona Howell, Belton Johnson, Mr. and Mrs. Paul Kearns, Mr. and Mrs. Richard "Dick" Kearns, Charlie Knapp,* Charlie Kohler, Mr.* and Mrs. Palmer Ladd.

Paul Ley, Mrs. Arnold Longmire, Charlotta Matthews, "Granny" Matthews,* Mrs. Gerald (Florence) Martin, Margaret Mickle, Stella Mitchell, Tom Mitchell, Mrs. John (Flora Woodring) Morris, Lettie "Miss Lettie" Nutt,* Andy Rosse, Clarence Rutland, Simeon Rouse, Philip Santini,* Mrs. Leon-

ard "Nell" Santini,* Arthur Schneider, Captain Ray Singleton, Oscar Sheets, Kent Smith, Jr., Kent Smith, Sr., Mrs. Jake
(Pearl) Stokes, Harry Stringfellow, George Thompson, Mrs.
Louise Waldron, Joe Wightman, Mr. and Mrs. W. M. Wiles,
and Esperanza Woodring.

In addition to these early homesteaders, settlers or visitors,
numerous governmental agencies have been of great help. The
U.S. Coast Guard, Seventh District, Lieutenant Commander
and Acting Chief, Public Information, J. W. Duenzl and L. K.
Thomas, Lieutenant (junior grade), were particularly cordial
in locating needed information about Light Houses.

Mark G. Eckhoff, Acting Director, Diplomatic, Legal, and
Fiscal Records Division, and William F. Sherman, of U.S. Archives and Records Service, Washington, D.C., were of assist-
ance in locating war records.

F. Kent Loomis, Captain, U.S.N. (Ret.), Assistant Director
of Naval History, Department of the Navy, was of great as-
sistance.

The Sanibel Public Library, Fort Myers Public Library, and
Florida State Library offered excellent service in early attempts to locate material.

Many scores of old-timers hunted out hundreds of photographs from their precious, long-hidden stores and loaned
them for use without question.

Bill Newman of the Sanibel Chamber of Commerce and
Norman Chambers of its board helped obtain the beautiful
color transparency from which the cover jacket was designed,
and Roland Q. Roberts of Fort Myers Beach (who owned
the color transparency) graciously allowed it to be used.

Lelia Morris Cunningham has labored many hours correct-
ing minor errors in copy and keeping enthusiasm up to complete the endless details and make history come alive.

So many have helped that one may be overlooked. If so, it
is an oversight and forgiveness is begged in advance for such
omission. The islands of yesterday deserve the best from all
and it is hoped that because of these stories and the wondrous cooperation of so many that the islands will continue
to be loved by future generations through the coming years.

Florence Fritz

Fort Myers, Florida
November 1968

x

Contents

PROLOGUE

PART I
From the Ice Age to the Light House

PART II
Of Homesteaders and Steamboats

PART III
Gay Slow Ferries Vs. Mainland Bridge

EPILOGUE

APPENDIX

Mrs. Flora Sanibel Woodring Morris—the first white child born on Sanibel Island. She married John E. Morris of Georgia in 1911. This picture was made in the year of her marriage.—Photo courtesy of Mrs. Morris

Sunset across the Gulf of Mexico: The sun going down this night would rise again tomorrow. The tides would ebb around these shores but they would flow in again. The stars and the moon followed their appointed paths in time—without need of the hands of man, without utterance of mortal words of "yea," or "nay." Such ever-present assurances gave island living a tranquillity never found on the mainland or in crowded cities of the earth.

Prologue

As you cross these sunlit waters . . .

You ride off from the mainland at Punta Rassa, leaving behind the mangrove jungles, coconut palms and cat's-claw black-bead vines, awed by the sunlit beauty of turquoise waters and continue over the modern white concrete bridges and low curving causeways.

Sometimes you note the young coconut palms growing on the white hot sands of the sloping roadsides. As your car climbs one of the bridges a flock of sea gulls may wheel and cry above in the bright blue sky.

At midday near one bridge in a small boat in the waters below, there may be a solitary fisherman leisurely lazing away the day.

Farther along a causeway, another fisherman will be standing hip-deep in the waters, casting forth his line, reeling it in, casting it again—oblivious to all but timeless time and peace.

Directly, you may notice the sign on the roadside that says: "Caution: BIRD CROSSING!"

You may wonder, "Why does a road department put up signs for birds that fly in the sky?"

Off to your left in the distance then you may observe the dark outline of Sanibel Light rising above the mangrove and buttonwood jungle. It blinks there, without fail, from sunset to dawn, as surely as the tides rise and fall, or the moon waxes and wanes. It stands on the point of the island that for centuries was known only as Point Ybel.

Point Ybel then was the focal point of history, landmark in the Western World for Conquistadores, for pirates, slavers, and warring men. For more than three-quarters of a century, since the Light was erected, it has warned seamen they were approaching the ancient "islands that jutted out into the sea."

In addition to history and warfare, around that shore and Light House there have been more happy gatherings and genuine good times than many villages and mainland towns know in all their years of being.

Puffs of white sunlit clouds waft lightly across the blue skies above, making small shadows on the waters and on the white silver sands. So insignificant are they that if you are driving a high-powered car you may not notice them. You may leave the causeway, spin hurriedly over the islands, and return—and go away wondering why anybody ever came here anyway.

How then will you learn that where now there are palm jungles once there were tomato farms? or that Cuban fishing smacks (licensed by the Captains-General of Cuba) used to lie to in hurricane time and up anchor to sail away later, leaving small gay memories behind? or that sailing ships and schooners—and later steamers (large and small)—sailed the waters of these islands? How will you guess that curiously interesting races and people have already been here—and gone?

The hurried, casual traveler usually visits the Light House on the point. Then, he rides over the islands, penetrating a few side trails, seeing tiny homeplaces hidden among coconut palms, exotic plants and flowers, and here and there, fronting the Gulf, a swank modern motel with a heated pool.

Along the abandoned ferry road, in a garden, he may be surprised to see a black iron kettle with three legs lying under a golden rain tree near a Hawaiian hibiscus bush, aglow with multi-colored flowers. That kettle once belonged to a homesteader and has a story of its own, but who is there to tell?

In summer, by the Coconut Grove Restaurant the mango tree from India may be heavily laden with luscious fruit. Beyond will be Bailey's Store (once Sanibel Packing Company). Across the way will be the new post office building above which flies the Stars and Stripes of the U.S.A.

But the stranger seldom knows that the road at this point once came up from a landing on Tarpon Bay and went to the

2

Gulf of Mexico; that over this road at infrequent intervals, or days, came a wagon or a carriage.

Such vehicles had carried produce to the steamer landing on the bay, or met an incoming traveler there. The settlers or visitors often walked behind the laden vehicle and sometimes they met an alligator crawling out from the marshes through which the old road ran.

Should you be of a poetic mind, you may vaguely realize that you are riding into history, hearing echoes of the past, feeling trade winds that still blow from the land of Yucatan and the Banks of Campeche.

If you are such a one, perhaps you may hear the faint daytime whistle and bell of steamboats on the bay, the sound of carefree children along the shore.

In the twilight, you may smile at the rasp of a fiddle and the stomp of mirthful gay parties at the Light House long ago; or dry a tear in the afterglow at the cry of a violin tuned to the sound of Gulf tides and the rhythm of the ages.

When the moon rises above the black mangrove jungles of surrounding islands, the campfires of the ancient ones may light again and you may hear the sounds of aborigines chanting to their God.

You may at length listen delightedly to a homesteader or seaman, now grown old, in some island bar, restaurant, or home, spinning yarns of yesterday. They will speak only of their own time, never knowing that before them for endless centuries there were other people and other ways and days.

Yet all of them will be fragments of the past of these islands, faint echoes coming down little paths of forgotten time.

You may walk the silver sands or pathways of shell and begin to wonder. "Who came here? Who went away? What happened long ago? Who is that shuffling old man trudging along like a phantom in the dusk?"

Is he Indian? Is he Spaniard? Ask him.

With a gentle shrug, he may pass on. But you may hear his soft answer coming back to you: "*¿Quién sabe, Señor*" (or Señora or Señorita, as the case may be), "*quién sabe?*"

Who knows? Who knows?

If you then linger here and slowly relax into the faraway, you will at last begin to see and feel and hear the songs of the old islands.

Returning to slow ways of tropic seas, meandering along paths beneath coconut palms, you will regain a sense of the limitlessness of space and time.

For these islands are lost places of the earth, set apart from the land, embraced forever by the sea, where clouds, winds, and tides are not and cannot be controlled by the hands of man.

You may lose your heart to these islands. If you do, you may eventually, as have many of those before you, try to hold back the outside world and all that the outside world has lost. . . .

Part I

FROM THE ICE AGE TO THE LIGHT HOUSE

Yesterday on these islands, towering against blue skies where white clouds drifted, grew sabal palms that had survived the Ice Age. In late spring, there were creamy-white blossom spikes of Spanish bayonets (*Yucca oloifolia*) and of palmettos (*little palms*). Crawling about over white sands in the shallows around the shores, huge horseshoe crabs, that had also survived the Ice Age, mated, as they had for eons, then disappeared into the sea.

Chapter 1

Island prelude to human history . . .

Sanibel and Captiva were barrier islands. They divided Pine Island Sound from the open Gulf of Mexico. Sometimes, they held back storm-tossed seas from the many islands that lay behind them in the shallow, saucer-like expanse of waters and islands. The first of these had been known to Europeans of the Old World for more than four hundred and fifty years. Aborigines had inhabited them for thousands of years. For eons before them, the islands had been known only to God.

During those unknown ages billions upon billions of minute shining particles of coral and rock had been grinding by the restless seas,[1] until at last they appeared like white, powdered sugar-sand, fringing the turquoise waters of the palm-fringed islands.

Sometimes the wide unbroken beaches were strewn almost knee-deep with exquisite seashells of fantastic shapes and colors—pink, yellow, brown, orange—and patterned with spots or zigzags, or spined with weird extensions. Some shone brightly and caught the rays of the sun, so they reflected light like bits of colored glass.

Offshore from the islands, beneath the Gulf waters, was the Floridian Plateau or Continental Shelf. It had been in existence for millions of years and had alternately, like the islands, been dry land or covered with shallow seas. Now it was a broad, nearly level, submerged shelf that sloped outward from the shores at the rate of less than three feet to the mile.[2]

Among the rocky hills and ledges of the Continental Shelf grew hundreds of thousands of mollusks. In the seaweeds and

7

sponges and among the undersea prairies as well as the ledges and hills, more than 200,000 varieties of mollusks built their seashell homes, mated, gave birth to young, found food, aged, and died.

And when the mollusks died, their beautiful homes were cast ashore with the endless tides to be seen eventually by men and marvelled at forever.

It was the Continental Shelf that tempered the climate of the islands so that raw easterly winds were unknown; westerly winds blew across the very fountainhead of the Gulf Stream and brought perennial warmth from the sea to the islands and shallow waters around them.

There was a rainy or wet season that lasted from June to September and a dry season that extended from October through April or May. Between June and November there were sometimes hurricanes.

When the great hurricanes blew, along with the wind-driven, foaming waters from the Yucatan and the Carib Sea, came trees, seeds, debris. Mollusks sometimes adapted themselves and their descendants still propagate their kind in these waters. Coconuts came ashore and took root. Strange tropical trees and plants came on logs and branches. Birds, flying before the winds, dropped seeds that found the islands to their liking and grew.

Sanibel Island lay in a curved, crescent shape in the waters, extending from east to northwest, its lower shore fronting south toward Yucatan and tides from the Carib Sea. The island was thirteen miles long and about three miles across at its widest part. Captiva Island lay in a north to south direction, as did most islands. It was about nine miles long and from nothing to three-quarters of a mile wide.[3]

But Sanibel became famous early because of its peculiar location as a landmark. Away from the Gulf, on the Sound and Bay, Sanibel's shores were smothered in mangrove jungle but these were penetrated by shallow bays, bayous, and inlets. From its eastern tip, up through the center, were three ancient shell ridges that paralleled the Gulf.[4] On these grew scattered sabal palm forests whose shaggy crowns continuously rustled in the sea winds against the bright blue sky.

8

Between the shining white beach and the ridges and palm forests were marshes that had natural drainage to outside waters. One, at least a half a mile wide, contained fresh water and was known to migrating wild birds that came each spring and fall. There were numerous prairies on the island and in the interior roamed deer, turkeys, rabbits, and quail.

While the seas had been grinding the bits of coral and rock into the silvery sands of the shores, downriver from the everglades interior with its rivers and streams came rich silt to enrich these warm shallow waters on their way to the open sea.

As a consequence, oyster bars formed to catch the nourishing silt as it passed. Oysters grew on the stilted roots of the mangrove jungles and were fed by the rise of the tides. Everywhere, in the warm shallow waters, billions of small sea lives were spawned and they became food for larger sea life to feed upon and in turn be eaten by others.

With the tides coming in through passes and channels from deep waters of the Gulf were giant jewfish, magnificent silver kings, monster devilfish, sawfish, sharks and sea turtles. Sometimes there were millions of silver or gray mullet, and schools of redfish, and bluefish.

Because there was so much food, high in the sky man-o'-war birds and eagles wheeled, pelicans and seabirds settled in island rookeries.

And, at some time lost in history, to these islands and abundant waters came people who later came to be called "mound people," or "pile dwellers," or "Caloosas." No one ever found for certain from where they came. Now they are gone from the islands and none is sure where.

Top, left: carved bone pin, with bird. Center, left: a pelican masquette of the Caloosas. Bottom of page, left, carved wooden figure of man; right, a tiny statuette of dark-colored, close-grained wood, thought to be a panther god; center, a deer masquette of wood, painted beautiful blue and white. Sometimes such masquettes had moveable ears and eyes. (Note: These carvings found by Frank Cushing, famous archeologist, were given wide publicity. His explorations at the same time of seventy-five mounds here, included in the same report, have never been given public recognition.)—Photos, Museum, University of Pennsylvania

Chapter 2

Shell mounds and pile dwellings . . .

Long before Sanibel and Captiva were named, long before
the Spaniards or French or English sailed these waters, the
islands were part of a far-flung kingdom of aborigines.

"South of the Caloosahatchee, at Miami and in the Big
Cypress they gave their name simply as *Kanyuksa Is-ti-tea-
ti.*"[1] Kanyuksa was the name of their country, *Is-ti-tea-ti*
meant red men. They were the red men of Kanyuksa.

Ponce called them Calos. Others named them Ka-la-sa or
Calusi. The English used Caloosa, but meanwhile, Fontenada
said they were Carlos people ruled by Carlos, which Menendez also called them. United States archeologist Frank Cushing[2] named them Pile Dwellers and Mound People.

Why Pile Dwellers? The fishing villages were constructed of
long, sturdy pilings, jettisoned down into the sea bottom at
the base of shell mounds. Platforms were fastened to the
pilings and on the platforms thatched homes were erected.

Rising above these Pile Dwellers' homes, the early islanders
had laboriously erected mounds (village foundations), of shell
and marl. Such material, exposed to air, came to resemble
cement. The mounds were rounded so that coastal winds
would not wear them away. Sometimes there were drainage
ways between the mounds.

Gumbo-limbo trees grew on the slopes and prickly-pear
cacti; some had gardens of a sort, according to one of the
early explorers. And atop each of these mound foundations
were built the chief's abode, the village storehouse, and its
temple. On the next lower levels were the thatched dwellings
of the servants of those at the top. Around the waters lived

11

the fishermen and their families in their pile dwellings on floating platforms.

There were avenue-like roadways from the lowest levels upward to the top. Up and down these the Red People came and went, busy with their ancient ways. When swirling tides tore at the pile dwellings below and the seas thundered in the wind, the people fled with their belongings to the sanctuary of temple and storehouse, hauling their canoes with them.

In the waters of the harbor, Sound, and Bay around Sanibel and Captiva long ago there were at least a hundred of these shell mound cities. Most of the time the open seas were so bright that they were the astonishing blue of babies' shining eyes or spring green like willows along the creek banks ashore.

When the mullet spawned in midwinter, the weather was warm and dry, and the fishing people made great hauls of the fish. They were cleaned, salted, and smoked under drying sheds of palm thatch where fires of buttonwood burned low. So were the roe, or eggs. Later the fish were stacked like stovewood under other drying sheds. All the while the air was permeated with the salt tang of the sea and the pleasant fragrance of smoking fish and roe.

The Indians used a shallow type of pirogue to navigate the inner waters of Bay, Sound, and River. For the open more dangerous Gulf waters, they had pirogues with high prows and woven sails that moved swiftly and safely over the seas.

Early Conquistadores occasionally found a great canoe, or a pair of them lashed together, propelled by sails of palm woven matting-like material. They would be transporting pottery, or dyed cloth, or trinkets of gold from the Antilles or Yucatan to the cities of the Pointed Land, or Caloosa.

The natives were "fine looking people" with reddish, copper-colored skin. They wore little clothing most of the year, as does modern man who dwells around the coast in summer. Breechclouts, a type of apron, made of exquisitely softened deer skin were worn by the men; the women wore neat garments that Conquistadores said resembled wood, which was woven from the fine hairs of Spanish moss. Necklaces and ornaments were made of shark teeth or small shells and bone.[3]

In their dwellings, mats were woven of palm fibers, as were baskets for gathering seeds and sweet berries to be dried. Their utensils were of wood or shell or bone—many of them beautifully carved in intricate designs.

Their children were treasured. Ball was played with great glee. And, in their primitive island world, the early inhabitants worshipped the Great Spirit of the Universe.

Like other native Americans, these islanders venerated the eagle, placing it atop totem poles in their villages on the mounds. They made remarkable replicas of the deer with movable ears and eyes, which were used for masks in some of their ceremonials. A design, some archeologists say is that of a spider, is more likely the under side of the great horseshoe crab—perhaps because it had survived the Ice Age and still lived on the shores.

Out in the Sound, across the way, they had built special temple mounds. There, around fires that cast a red glow in the darkness of sub-tropic nights, the Indians held religious observances; which, to them, were probably as sacred as ours are to us.

Moreover, they respected their dead, burying them in specially built mounds which were usually made of sand. Around the mounds they made water highways lined with seashells so they might reach them by canoe.

As late as 1895, on one of the inner marginal reefs of Sanibel Island,[4] "the lower end of which formed . . . a great loop around the Bay," there were remains of mounds. Well defined canals led in from among shell-bank enclosures within a mangrove swamp to a built up point terminating in a diminutive court.

When Frank Cushing, the famous Zuni explorer and U.S. archeologist, dug into the middle of one of the terraces from the outer shore he found "not only numerous relics, but also large flat fragments of breccia-like cement."[5]

Higher up, on the more level portion of this terrace, Cushing found that the cement was continuous over a considerable space, but "that the bed this formed ended abruptly

13

along a line parallel with the western edge or end of the elevation."

At almost regular intervals along this line, Cushing found holes in the "compact substratum of shell, formed by the decaying of stout posts that had been set therein" as was shown by the lingering traces of rotten wood that occurred in each.

It appeared to this expert, that this flat bed of cement had once formed a thin vertical wall or rather the plastering of a timber-supported wall, probably the end of some large building which had crowned the terrace, and that had fallen in under the stress of some storm or as a result of some other accident, which may well have been destruction by the Spanish invaders.

Also on Sanibel there was a long, very low sandspit, comparatively narrow, and covered with mangroves which extended in a direction parallel with the curved inner shores, . . . from very near the end of this ancient settlement to almost the end of the island itself. This low bar, joined by another that put out from the oppositely curved shore enclosed a round body of water known as Ellis' Bay.[6]

When Cushing heard that Captain Ellis had found some human bones near his quaint palmetto huts on the southern shore of the Bay, he made a visit there, describing it thus:

"The thatched houses irregularly set on the low flat stretch of sand, amid clumps of native palmettoes and luxuriant groves of lime, orange, and other tropical fruit trees"[7] were picturesque indeed. Captain Ellis was whole-souled in courtesy and helpfulness during the prosecution of Cushing's hasty excavations there.

Behind this above "assemblage of huts, the land rose gradually to a considerable height, consisting almost wholly of sea sand, that had been drifted over from the opposite beaches of the Gulf. This sand drift had, in the course of centuries, quite buried a low but extensive ancient settlement.

"A drainage canal, that had recently been dug by settlers living farther up the island, revealed to me the previously unsuspected presence of this settlement, and the fact that it,

14

Totem and pottery

Like many American Indians, the island aborigines venerated the American eagle. Thousands of fragments of pottery, both red and black, have been found over the years on Sanibel and Captiva. Pottery designs were often formed by rows of small tick marks, which usually formed simple chevron or running-V designs.— Pottery from *The Florida Anthropologist*[8]

like all the others I have described, had been built up originally from reefs and shoals.

"From it a sort of causeway of conch-shells had once led out toward a nearly round, enclosed space, closer to the present shore, and off to the westward side of Ellis' place. This enclosure is now (1895), of course, filled with boggy muck and overgrown; but it surrounded a somewhat extensive, low mound, composed in part of shells and in part of black soil.

"The . . . mound was under cultivation as a vegetable and fruit garden; and it was in the attempt to remove from it the roots of a large stump, that Captain Ellis had made the find of human bones. . . . In excavating near by, I discovered that the whole heap was permeated . . . with broken human remains; large bones and small, many of which had been split or shattered, mingled with skulls, some few fortunately still entire, although very fragile. I succeeded in securing eleven of these skulls before leaving. . . ."

If the silver sands and shells of the outer beaches told the secrets of the ancient seas, so the mangrove jungles of the inner Bay shores of Sanibel and Captiva held and still hold secrets of the ancient people.

Historians, archeologists, and ethnologists fail to agree as to the origin of the people of the islands. Some say the people came from China eons ago.

Nor is there agreement as to when they arrived. Some scientists now believe the mounds and inhabitants have been in existence more than twenty-five hundred years.

Because the mound people, or pile dwellers, were used to the sea and its ways, that and many other ideas point to the warm southern seas as their original home. There are still mounds such as those of these islands, along the coast of South America as far as Brazil.

They could readily have come up from the Carib seas when the ancient land bridge still connected the Florida Keys with the Yucatan peninsula eons ago. They could more likely have found their way up from the Carib seas after the Ice Age and gradually built their shell mounds on these islands and around these shores as the waters melted and rose and as hurricanes taught them further need.

One thing is certain: In the shallow waters around the islands, these Red People lived in their palm-thatched dwellings on and around the shell mounds[9] and laughed and loved, unmolested, for thousands of tranquil years.

It was so when Juan Ponce de Leon sought them and the islands that "jutted out into the sea," and found the "garden cities" of these waters when he arrived more than 450 years ago.

The approach of armor-clad Spanish soldiers caused panic among the pile dwellers and mound people. Their twelve-foot long "pikes" served as extended bayonets and were used, as they charged, to impale unruly victims. Horses of the Conquistadores had metal head coverings with eyeholes in them, which added to the terror as the invaders rode up the ancient ways of Indian villages, scattering people right and left for sport.—Sketch from a museum display by Eleanor D. Clapp

18

Chapter 3

Ybel y Cautivo and Pedro Menendez . . .

There were clouds over the Gulf and shadows on the sea that day when Ponce de Leon sailed from this pointed land. Why he ever stopped on the east coast remains a mystery, unless he mistrusted information given by Indians who had been questioned and thought he might there find a southern harbor that did not exist.

Admittedly, Ponce was seeking "the islands that jutted out into the sea, the first of which lay east and west in the Gulf of Mexico like Cuba in the Caribbean."[1] He had learned of this well-forested Indian nation where there were mineral springs, plenty of wild animals and fine coastal fisheries—and gold that he could take to add to his fortune.

As his ships ploughed the bright blue waters around the tip of the pointed land from east to west, he named places along the route. There was no water but plenty of turtles on one island group, so he named them the *Tortugas.* He named one bay after himself but no one has ever been sure which bay it was.

It might have been Tortugas Harbor; it may have been Florida Bay; it could have been *Esenada de Caloosa (Carlos),* for in the great basin of Caloosa or Carlos Bay (now called Charlotte Harbor and San Carlos Bay), lay the capital cities of the ancient Caloosa nation.

Ponce sailed from Tortugas on a north by east course and came to the islands that jutted out into the sea. The first island lay east and west with a white glistening beach that fronted toward far away Havana. Its eastern point was toward a broad river that was the water highway connecting

19

with the Indian provinces of the interior; the point also marked the southern entrance to the capital cities.

As he stood at the threshold of conquest, was it not logical that Ponce should name this lovely point after Isabella? True, Isabella (born 1451, the daughter of King John II, of Castile and Leon, consort of Ferdinand, the Catholic King) had died in 1505. But Ferdinand was still on the throne. Surely it was good politics for exuberant Ponce to name this most important landmark in his conquest of the new continent after the late powerful queen!

The name appeared thereafter on maps and in records spelled Y Bel, Ybel, Isabella, San Y Bel, San Ybel, Sanybel, Senybel, Sanabal, Sannybal. At last it became Sanibel, and although it is still Point Ybel, the entire island is Sanibel.

It is a safe bet that as Ponce, according to his diary, sailed up the coast from Point Ybel he named Ciego (Blind) Pass. Not far from there, Ponce "discovered a great deep bay, of sufficient size for many ships, which had a depth of thirty-one feet. He sailed on a short distance beyond, then turned back, entered the *Bahia Hondo* (Deep Bay) and moved into the sound where the great cities of the Caloosas lay. He dropped anchor and sent out boats to examine the island villages and surrounding waters.

Then, says Barcia, "there was a battle" and Ponce and his ships "returned whence they came."[2] Other reports speak of bloody battles, for which Matanzas Pass across from Sanibel is named, meaning murder or bloodshed. One thing is sure, Ponce reported to Havana and returned to Puerto Rico quite satisfied with his new conquest and sure that his "discoveries" would eventually bring him good fortune.

Of the various reasons given for this voyage, it is most probable that Ponce intended to and did capture Indians for the slave markets of the Antilles, and this was what precipitated the battle that sent him home wounded. At least one record states that on June 14, Ponce and his men returned to "Hispañola, taking captives with them."

Therefore, it can well be assumed that, at that time, *Passeo Cautivo* (Pass of captive or prisoner) was applied to Captiva Pass and later the name applied to the island. Passes or *esenadas* (entrances) were then of great importance. Through them ships found their way from the Gulf to the inside calmer waters during sudden storms. Through them invading ships could send long boats to surround one or more of the smaller island villages, overpower the unsuspecting inhabitants, and take them away to become slaves in the Spanish mines of the Caribbean islands.

In later centuries, a legend of girl captives of pirates living on the island was said to be the meaning of Captiva yet old maps show that the island was so named long before the legend was concocted.

After this first visit of Ponce de Leon, the maps of the world were changed forever. Ybel, Boca Ciego, Cautivo, and many other names became part of written history. The sun-swept coastal islands and translucent, sea-green waters remained around Ybel and Cautivo but the peace of the islands was to be no more.

Before Ponce there had been other Spanish visitors for the aborigines understood the Spanish language and fought desperately against subjection. Now others came. Diego Miruelo operated a caravel between Cuba and Florida; Cordova explored; so did Alonza Alvarez de Pineda. All were bent on slavery, conquest, profits.

Their comings and goings to the land Ponce considered his own by right of "discovery" alarmed him. Moreover, King Philip II had ascended the Spanish throne and Ponce's future in Puerto Rico looked dark. In 1521, Ponce de Leon recalled that seven years before King Ferdinand had granted him a royal patent to Florida. This he hastily took up and sailed for the pointed land and the islands that jutted out into the sea.[3]

This time, he fetched mares, heifers, sheep, goats, all kinds of seeds, 250 men and 50 horses. To "civilize" the Caloosas, he brought monks and priests.[4] He intended to colonize and conquer.

His expedition landed nearby but there is no record stating whether he entered Caloosa through the northern or southern entrance—through Charlotte Harbor or Carlos Bay. Certainly he passed Point Ybel, but the livestock aboard the ships

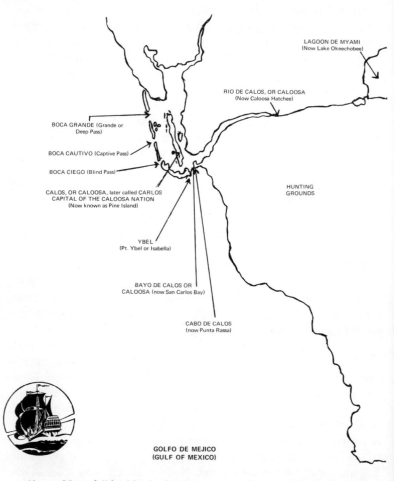

LAGOON DE MYAMI
(Now Lake Okeechobee)

RIO DE CALOS, OR CALOOSA
(Now Caloosa Hatchee)

BOCA GRANDE (Grande or
Deep Pass)

BOCA CAUTIVO (Captive Pass)

BOCA CIEGO (Blind Pass)

CALOS, OR CALOOSA, later called CARLOS
CAPITAL OF THE CALOOSA NATION
(Now known as Pine Island)

HUNTING
GROUNDS

YBEL
(Pt. Ybel or Isabella)

BAYO DE CALOS OR
CALOOSA (now San Carlos Bay)

CABO DE CALOS
(now Punta Rassa)

GOLFO DE MEJICO
(GULF OF MEXICO)

Above: Map of "the islands that jut out into the sea and lie in the Gulf of Mexico like Cuba in the Caribbean Sea"; and Point Ybel and island passes that for many decades were the focal point of history.

Inside these outer islands lay what is now Pine Island, capital of the Calos or Caloosa Nation, which consisted of many provinces and people of southern Florida, whom Ponce de Leon came to invade and conquer.

And Point Ybel was the landmark that marked the entrance to the Capital.

22

needed to be landed ashore rather than on an island because of the need for grazing and water.

It is probable, but unproved, that he landed at Punta Rassa or across Carlos Bay at Sword Point. They were on the mainland where a colony could have been established to serve as a beachhead from which to conquer the interior as well as the islands of the Caloosa Nation.

As Ponce's expedition unloaded, the Caloosas attacked them in great fury. Once again, Ponce was wounded. The unhappy expedition hurriedly debarked and returned to Cuba intending to return when Ponce recovered. But Ponce died and with him his dream of conquering the Caloosa Nation.

It was eighteen years before the next invaders passed Point Ybel. First came Narvaez (1529), then de Soto (1539). Historians familiar with the geography of the Gulf Coast generally agree that both Narvaez' expedition, which ended in disaster, and de Soto's invasion, which also ended in tragedy, came up the Gulf to Point Ybel and entered the ports of Carlos—either through the southern entrance by Point Ybel into Carlos Bay, or into the northern entrance, now called Charlotte Harbor.

Although these expeditions were said to have followed in the footsteps of Ponce de Leon, few historians today agree just where the landings were. In 1939, in an effort to settle the dispute for all time, the United States National de Soto Commission was established.[5] It published a ponderous book, yet, in the end, after three years' work the commission concluded its findings by saying it wasn't sure of anything.

Adding to the confusion is the fact that in 1771 Bernard Romans, a Dutch surveyor for the British government, claimed he discovered a great bay and named it Charlotte Harbor. He was in error.

Actually, there were two "deep bay" entrances to the old Caloosa Nation. The southern bay, nearest Cuba, was Carlos or Caloosa Bay, the northern one Romans gave an English name. The two bays through which entrance was gained to the capital cities of the Nation, were connected by Pine Island Sound and Matlacha Pass. The deep water channel of the Sound was navigable for large ships with experienced pilots.

The important fact to remember is that Point Ybel and Sanibel were the first landmarks for mariners coming up from the south. Therefore, they became the focal point of New World history, and Western World beginnings, more than half a century prior to the settlement of Saint Augustine (although the latter is the oldest permanent settlement in Florida).

The last big effort to conquer the Pile Dwellers and Mound People was by Pedro Menendez de Aviles.[6] He first established a toehold of a colony on the Florida east coast, calling it Saint Augustine. Then, in 1566 he approached these islands, entering through the northern port of Carlos. (Other Spaniards had, meanwhile, changed the name of the great chief, as well as that of the people and their islands, to "Carlos," honoring King Charles V of Spain and intending to impress the natives with the power of that ruler across the seas.)

Menendez came with the blessings of the Spanish Crown, "to pacify the southern coast, locate a harbor necessary as a port of refuge around the southern coast, and to protect shipwrecks of treasure ships and galleons."

During the next couple of years, Pedro Menendez returned several times. He used both force and cajolery to bring about an alliance. Between visits, he left Jesuit priests to remain on the islands, convert the people, and establish colonies of religious natives among them.

Pedro had much to lose if his efforts to subdue Carlos failed. Had he succeeded, the king had already agreed he could keep almost everything he could take in his conquest. In addition, he was granted (even before taking them), two fisheries; twenty-five square leagues of land; one or two towns; and other considerations.

Eventually, Pedro had to anchor in Carlos Bay off Point Ybel because he "dared not again enter the great bay northward" where lived the "fiercest defenders of the Carlos capital."

So, what to do? In this land of white sugar-sands, where

24

schools of fish were so vast they made roaring sounds as they passed and where people had once dwelt in peace—Menendez had the chiefs of eighteen of the embattled provinces of Carlos rounded up at the capital across from Ybel, and there they were beheaded.

Chapter 4

Missionaries, pescadores, *and pirates . . .*

After Pedro Menendez had departed from this land of sunlit waters and island villages, and the chiefs of Carlos were dead, the Spaniards remained farther north and began to venerate their New World beachhead city, Saint Augustine. For the most part, the Caloosa or Carlos Nation was forgotten. But not quite.

There never was a time that Point Ybel did not know the sight of colored sails and three-decked treasure ships lumbering down the Gulf shore, carrying loot from the Mexican Aztecs and Mayans and the South American Incas. From near Sanibel in the Gulf they sailed south by southwest toward the Tortugas and Havana. Later, guarded by men-of-war, they sailed for Spain.

Nor was there ever a long period of time when missionaries failed to come to these islands.

Circa 1680, when the Franciscans had become successful in establishing Catholic missions across upper Florida, another attempt was made to enter Carlos. Around Point Ybel to the *pescadores grandes* came Juan Rodiquez de Cartayo. Unfortunately, the Spanish governor issued orders forbidding the island dwellers to play their favorite game, ball. Cartayo was forced to withdraw, abandoning the missions.

In 1695, two priests working in Carlos were disrobed and taken by Indians down to the Florida Keys to the Catholic settlement of Matecumbe.

Thereafter, for three years, the aborigines were not allowed to trade with Cartegena from their port of Toempe on Charlotte Harbor. At the end of the three-year penalty, after

26

they had agreed to allow friars to work in their provinces, the ports of Carlos were once more opened for trade.[1]

In the meantime, over the years, some fishermen and coastal traders became converts or were married to Christians. These became known as Spanish Indians. Other Indians moved farther south among the lower coastal villages or retired to the upriver provinces or around the lake.

Then Governor Don Juan Maruez Carrera attempted to remove the remaining Indians from the coastal islands and many Catholic Indians were killed; others were carried away to become slaves.

It had long been a custom for Spaniards to make surprise raids around Point Ybel and Cautivo to capture natives. Had not Christopher Columbus established slavery in the West Indies on his second voyage? For about three hundred years the aborigines had been fighting for their freedom and it was becoming a losing battle.

By 1708 there was a slave route around Point Ybel, from deep water via smaller boats up the Caloosa Hatchee, across Lake Mayami (Okeechobee) and northern Florida to the English colonies. It mattered little to the pirates and slavers whether their cargoes were African or Indian.

Sometimes Spaniards, Frenchmen, or Englishmen captured each other's ships and fought and killed the crews. The people of the islands became impartial, taking any or all, holding some Frenchmen and Spaniards for ransom or death, enjoying the wreckage of the ships as it pleased them.

In later years, it was greedy men of the world on the high seas (who left no records, only legends undoubtedly based upon fact) that were the cruel outlaws who became the smugglers and slavers.

There came a time when Great Britain swapped Catholic Cuba to Spain in exchange for Florida, and divided it into *East* and *West* Florida. Almost a century prior to this the Spanish governor had ordered coastal Indians from the islands to the interior. Island fisheries, that had not been destroyed by burning, were expropriated and operated by Indian converts and their retinues. Many of these Catholic Spaniards now departed for Havana, not wishing to live under

27

Protestant rule, and the other Indians returned to their fisheries.

Great Britain allowed "the Indians of the Southern Provinces" of Florida to trade as they wished. Indian fisheries prospered once more. *Ybel* and *Cautivo* were more or less forgotten, except for the visit of Bernard Romans.

Romans, a Dutch surveyor, was sent, *circa* 1771, to survey the Floridas for Great Britain.[2] During his journey along the Gulf coast of East Florida, he renamed some bodies of water, and examined and wrote about the islands and fisheries of the region.

The fisheries[3] were located on islands inside the northern and southern entrances to the harbor of old Carlos. They were clusters of neat, well-thatched homes and had extensive sheds for drying fish and storehouses to hold salt and provisions.

Indians who operated them cultivated clearings in which they raised corn, pumpkins, and melons. Men, women, and children were engaged in the fishing operations. They used seines of woven palmetto, and floats of heavy seashells.

Attached to the fisheries were small fishing smacks that were licensed by the captain general of Cuba. The dried, salted fish and roe were sold in the Havana markets.

"Here," Romans wrote, "is Carlos Bay and the Caloosa Hatchee . . . with the island of San Ybel, where we find the southern entrance of Charlotte Harbor. . . ."

On a map accompanying his book, Romans showed Carlos Bay, the island of San Ybel, Boca Captiva, Boca Cego (Ciego?), Carlos Harbor, and the Caloosa Hatchee. Yet, at the same time, he claimed he had "discovered a large river, which empties itself into the new harbour, of which I am the first explorer."[4]

He gave it the name of *"Charlotte Harbour,"* because, he said, "neither harbour nor river have been described by the Spaniards on their maps." Since that time, historians have invariably called the northern entrance to Carlos *"Charlotte Harbor,"*[5] ignoring the fact that the waters had been known for 258 years prior to the coming of Romans.

No matter how you consider this, you will be obliged to

puzzle over how Romans discovered one body of water and named it, yet used the ancient Spanish and Indian nomenclature for all the others.[6] Also you will wonder why historians have called the northern entrance to Carlos Harbor "Charlotte Harbor," and ignored the history of previous centuries.

Small wonder that the story of Ybel and the islands became confused and lost to history.

When Spain regained Florida in 1783 she was weak and poor and few Catholics returned to these islands. The Spanish-Indians and Indians were unmolested. Pirates of many nations, however, found the channels deep and the islands a haven from which to prey upon ships from anywhere that came this way.

Tales about LaFitte, Blackbeard, Black Caesar, Black Augustus, and Gasparilla remain like imaginary evil phantoms in morning mists among island palms.

According to David True,[7] Black Caesar made his home on the high Sanibel shell mounds of the Bay and old rumor insists that José Gasparilla kept female prisoners on lovely Captiva Isle.

As the story goes, Caesar was an escaped slave, born of a half-Scotch father and a Negro mother. He joined the pirates and "worked his way up." At last, he made a great haul of twenty-six tons of silver bars from a ship on the open seas. Fetching his loot ashore, he buried it on one of the keys south of Miami at the place called Caesar's Creek, and let his ship be destroyed by hurricane winds and waves.

When settlers began to arrive along that coast, Caesar grew nervous. He moved to the forgotten West Coast, where, from atop the high, lonely mounds, he could keep watch on both Gulf and Bay.

But he could not hide forever. Trailing him was the widow of a Baltimore preacher. She sought vengeance because her husband's eyes had been burned out by the pirate. She located him on Sanibel, notified authorities, and had her day.

Black Caesar was caught, whipped, bound, and taken by sea to Key West. There he was tied to a tree and burned to death—the fire under him being lit by the widow herself.

Details as to how the widow found the pirate on Sanibel are not explained. Why the U.S. Caribbean Squadron would allow the whipping and burning has never been questioned. Pirate tales cannot be substantiated anymore than one can grasp the mists of morning in one's hands.

This is also true about José Gaspar.

Some say Gaspar lived on Gasparilla Island and buried his gold and silver treasures on Sanibel—or Useppa, or up the rivers or streams hard by. He kept lovely lady captives on Captiva Island, villains of the skull and crossbones guarding them until Gaspar called. And their wails rose in the lonely nights of the despair.

Once Gaspar captured a Spanish princess with a cluster of Mexican Indian girls on their way by ship to Spain for religious education. He divided the Mexican Indian maidens among his men. The Spanish princess he selected for himself.

To his misfortune, Gaspar fell in love with his princess. She virtuously spurned his love, until at last he had her royal head chopped off (before his very eyes) and buried her body on lovely Captiva Island.

She haunted him, some say, until the day he died and her remains lie buried on the island somewhere in an unmarked grave. Gaspar lost heart and was tracked down by a vessel of the West Indian Squadron in these waters.

The favorite ending is that when Gaspar aboard his ship saw the enemy approaching, he clanked an anchor chain around his legs and jumped overboard to his doom. He lies in the waters of the Pass, beyond the island where his beloved lies.

There are several things to remember, however. The island of Gasparilla was so named even before Romans came to make his survey. The name José is Spanish, but Gaspar is Italian. The United States did not seriously war on West Coast pirates until about 1824.

José was surely an old man for such young ideas, but then again *¿quién sabe?*

Who knows?

Chapter 5

Sanybel, sugarcane, and soldiers . . .

The Indians of the islands were not concerned about the pirates. They were content with the teeming waters and wild birds and freedom. Far away, unknown to them, Florida became a territory of the United States and in 1822 Sanibel and Captiva and all Charlotte Harbor waters became the responsibility of the Key West District for the U.S. Collector of Customs.

That year, Congress appointed Commodore David Porter, U.S. Navy, to command the West Indian Squadron against the pirates, and two years later, Porter sent Commander James McIntosh, in command of the schooner *Terrier,* to check the fisheries of Carlos Bay and Charlotte Harbor.

By that time, remaining Spaniards and Indians had intermarried until their religion was no longer a quarreling point. Also, the United States-Spain agreements had guaranteed religious freedom and American citizenship to the inhabitants of the *Spanish Ranchos,* or fisheries.[1]

Moreover the United States, in its plans for Constitutional government, had separated Church and State forever: It wanted no more European quarrels over such matters. And in 1823, under its Monroe Doctrine, the young new nation had announced its famous policy: that the American continents were to be no longer subjects for colonization by any European power.

So Commodore Porter sent Commander McIntosh and the schooner *Terrier* to examine Charlotte Harbor islands for pirates and whatever might be there.

There were far fewer Indian villages than in Ponce's time, or Menendez'. It was similar to the time of Romans.

At the mouth of the Caloosa Hatchee and around Sanibel, Captiva, and other islands there were the fisheries. They were made up of neat, well-thatched homes, fish drying sheds, storehouses for salt and provisions and on the shell mounds were clearings in which grew corn, pumpkins, and melons.

McIntosh found no evidence of piracy, only smoke from small cook fires on the breccia-like cement "stoves" of the aborigines and odors of cooking wafting across the blue waters in the warm trade winds. All was at peace around the islands. McIntosh went away again.

When William A. Whitehead, the Key West Collector of Customs, sailed up from that place in 1831 to check the fisheries he found four of them around Sanibel and Captiva. Half of the inhabitants were Indians. Thirty were women. Fifty or a hundred were children. The men were away fishing.

Since their vessels regularly entered and cleared Key West and paid tonnage duty and bought some supplies, Whitehead could find no fault and he sailed on, leaving them in peace.

In 1833 a large house and several smaller ones were erected on Point Ybel so that newcomers could hunt and fish, and a crop of sugarcane was raised on Sanibel. The following year, under Florida Territorial Acts of 1833, two settlements were incorporated for Sanibel by men named William Bunce, Colonel D. Murray (of New York), W. R. Hackley, and P. B. Prior.[2]

This same year, in March, Prior and others made a trip "through the Indian country to the mouth of the Sanybel River (Caloosa Hatchee)."[3] They had a pilot of their sloop, a Mexican Indian named Greig, to lead them through Charlotte Bay (Harbor).

The sloop sailed inside the islands. They found passages "north of Sanybel: the first, Bocca Seca (Boca Ciego), Bocca Captiva, and Bocca Grand."

Twenty-five miles from "Punta Raza" (Punta Rassa) they made the island inhabited by the Calde family which contained from fifty to sixty inhabitants.[4] On the same key,

32

they found a Mr. Willis, inspector of customs, who was building a house on the north end of the key.

On this journey the sloop stopped at many keys and found them under cultivation, producing Cuba corn, pumpkins, melons, potatoes (yams), various kinds of beans, and other vegetables and fruits.

It was found that the inhabitants of these waters lived on "fish, turtles, and coontie [this last brought from the mainland]"; they had "some coconut trees in bearing, oranges, limes, papayas, haweys, and hickok plums [coco plums]."[5]

Murray, Hackley, and Prior visited Carlos Bay again in a small sloop, the *Associate,* in 1837 with Captain Bunce. This time they visited Cayo Pueblo which was inhabited by Spanish and Indians, and proceeded to "ascend the bay."[6]

They anchored near another fishing *rancho* and then sailed on. The channel became narrow, crooked, difficult to locate. They ran aground on oyster shoals. So, they returned to the *rancho.*

This "bay" was the Sanibel entrance to Carlos Bay and the lower Caloosa Hatchee. "It appeared," John Lee Williams wrote, "to be a large stream but has never been explored. . . ." He also said: "No writer has described this region since the change of flags," but that was in 1819.

Another writer, named Lawson sailed the coast and announced these islands "altogether uninhabitable. . . ."

But Williams said "Sanybel" was twelve miles long and about two wide. On its margin there were some narrow hammocks. On its point was a fine harbor, "varying from two to four fathoms, with fourteen feet on the bar." "On this island" he wrote, "there are streams of fresh water." It is about "eight feet above the highest tides, and is dry and healthy, and almost constantly refreshed with sea breezes."

"Capativa" (Captiva) extended about seven miles down the coast.

Apparently Williams wrote his impressions over a period of years. In 1837, he said that "the elegant house" and several smaller ones that had been built in 1832 on Sanibel, were "nearly deserted." A few pages farther on he said: "Several

33

buildings were erected here . . . before the Seminole War commenced, all are now destroyed. . . ."

There was good reason for these events: For decades, the United States had been trying to persuade Seminole Indians of upper Florida to emigrate west. Instead, the Seminoles had fled south into the land of the Caloosas. The soldiers had followed.

Now, though silver kings rolled in the blue waters around the islands and an occasional sea turtle lifted its ungainly head above the surface of the waters, the U.S. Steamer *Iris* came sailing around Point Ybel and anchored near old *Cabo de Carlos* (Punta Rassa).

Soldiers busily went about near the fishing villages there. They built a dock and a fort they called Fort Dulaney. Soldiers operated from there up the ancient Caloosa Hatchee and among the coastal shell-mound villages. The Spanish ranchos, suspected of disloyalty to the "cause," were "scoured" by the military. Thatched villages were burned. The inhabitants were taken prisoner, if they survived, and transported west, as "Seminoles."

Two years later, May 18, 1839, Major General Macomb[7] held a parley with some Indians and issued a general order claiming the war "with the Seminole Indians" was at an end. Those remaining on the mainland were to move to a reservation. It would begin "at the most southern point of land between *Charlotte Harbor and the Sanybel or Caloosahatchee River opposite Sanybel Island,*[8] thence to Charlotte Harbor by the southern pass between Pine Island and that point, along the eastern shore . . ." of the mainland, etc.

This "treaty" excluded all the islands but roughly embraced all the mainland of present southwestern Florida. No Indians were to leave the limits assigned to them; U.S. troops would see that the area was not intruded by citizens or foreigners; Indians had two moons during which to remove possessions from the coast to the interior.

Two months later, to Sanibel Island[9] came twenty-five dragoons, Lieutenant Colonel W. J. Harney and a party that included a Sutler, Dahlman, Morgan, Dahlman's English clerk, two laborers, a carpenter, a Negro named Sampson, and Captain H. McCarty, pilot.

One day, they all boarded sloops and sailed from Sanibel, across Carlos Bay, and up the Caloosa Hatchee—into the heart of the new Indian reservation.

Opposite the large mound villages where now Fort Myers stands, the soldiers and civilians unloaded supplies and equipment and soon had a Sutler's store built and temporary encampment made. Pirogues of Indians crossed to the north shore and silently went away, but the night found campfires lit, war dances, and war cries, which were not noticed by the new settlement.

In the rose dawn many Indians attacked, killing soldiers and civilians alike. Colonel Harney and some men got away and angrily made their way back to Sanibel.[10]

It was apparent that the ancient mound people and pile dwellers had joined with the Seminoles, and "war" commenced again. Around Point Ybel to Carlos Bay across to Fort Dulaney there were comings and goings of the military of the United States. Supplies were unloaded there for transshipment upriver to other little forts. Soldiers and sailors came from the Florida east coast or down from Fort Brook (Tampa) or from Fort King (Gainesville). Mound villages and interior hideaways were sought out, burned, and inhabitants taken prisoners to be sent west.

In the end, there was peace once more. The same boundaries previously mentioned were reaffirmed. But the island Indians were legally shut away from their natural haunts forever.

Top: U.S.S. *Hibiscus*, part of the East Gulf Blockading Squadron during the War Between the States. Below: U.S.S. *Isonomia*, a side-wheel steamer, also part of the nine-vessel flotilla that steamed up the Gulf Coast and left the *Restless*, and the *Two Sisters*, on duty to patrol Carlos Bay and Charlotte Harbor. No picture of the *Restless* or *Two Sisters* was available at the time of this printing.—U.S. Navy official photos

Chapter 6

Sisal, another war, and castor beans . . .

While these Indian "wars" were going on, over on Indian Key Dr. Henry Perrine had introduced *Agave sisalina Perrine* from Yucatan and planted it near various Indian settlements before he was massacred. During those wars, fast sailing sloops and schooners had been sailing by Sanibel and Captiva. They carried cotton cargoes from Mobile and New Orleans to eastern ports of the United States and fetched back furbelows and supplies to the rich plantations of the upper Gulf coast.

These translucent waters, the multitudes of birds, even the islands seemed deserted by man, but this was not so. Spanish Indians had returned here and there. A few other Spaniards had come to avoid conscription into the armies of Spain. Occasionally a sloop or small schooner would lay to and quietly drop anchor in a bay or bayou, and never go away any more.

Among the unknown island dwellers of that period were some planters of sisal hemp, or henequen (*Agave sisalina*), the profitable fiber of Yucatan. They also planted the bowstring hemp (*Sansevieria*—commonly known as rattlesnake lily or spotted lily), wild pineapple or *bromelia sylvestria* that was extensively used in Mexico for the manufacture of hammocks, nets, and cordage, the common pineapple, and the ramie.

A full report of these plantings on Sanibel appears in the United States Agriculture Department's report of 1856.[1] Yet no names of the experimenters are known, nor are details revealed as to what happened to the crops. Today, however,

37

all over the islands are descendants of these growing wild under the sun, reminding those who know of the mute story of long ago island dwellers' dreams.

The next available news of Sanibel and Captiva began five years later when war came again to the islands.[2] From 1861 to 1865 the fast sailing sloops and schooners with their rich cargoes that had been sailing the coast offshore from Point Ybel, came no more.

Federal soldiers held Key West to the south and other coastal points to the north. Isolated Sanibel and Captiva still knew the flocks of birds and schools of fish on spring and fall migrations. Trade winds wafted over the thatched villages of the islands. The harbors nearby belonged to anybody, but the Federals did not know it yet.

"Cuba libre!" cried Cuban refugees during that time, as they made one of their sporadic attempts to free themselves from Spain, and arrived in Key West. Shortly, the Federals suspected them of collaborating with the Confederates. Their possessions were confiscated and the Cubans banished from Key West. Some of them sailed up the west coast and quietly became settlers on lonely islands.

All the while over on the mainland, Captain McKay had been supplying the Confederacy with cattle, driving herds up through the state to near the Georgia line. He now reached a decision that the South was going to lose the war and joined forces with Jacob (Jake) Summerlin to sell cattle to the Spanish government.

McKay and Summerlin drove wild cattle to old *Cabo de Carlos* which became known as Punta Rassa or Cattle Point, across from Sanibel. The cattle were loaded on schooners in Carlos Bay and delivered to Havana. On return trips contraband supplies were brought to Confederates living on the islands and around Charlotte Harbor and up the Caloosa Hatchee.

As the war neared its close, in early 1865, Captain James Doyle with his 110th New York Negro Infantry, which was composed of ex-slaves, moved upriver from Punta Rassa to try to capture wild cattle to furnish beef for their commissary. Confederate soldiers from Fort Thompson, up the Caloosa Hatchee, attacked Doyle's group. And this provoked a crisis for the Federals thus learned about McKay and Summerlin's activities around Carlos Bay.

From Key West, Brigadier General John Newton[3] and his headquarters staff embarked in the side-wheel gunboat U.S.S. *Honduras,* with acting volunteer Lieutenant Harris commanding, and companies A, B, and K of the Second U.S. Colored Infantry aboard—destination Punta Rassa and the upper west coast. The date was February 25, 1865. There were nine ships in the flotilla.

A camp was established at Point Ybel, also at Punta Rassa, and on the tip of Pine Island. The fisheries of Carlos Bay and those around the mouth of the Caloosa Hatchee were destroyed. When he departed, the brigadier general left the bark U.S.S. *Restless,*[4] with acting volunteer Lieutenant W. P. Randall commanding, to patrol "the Charlotte Harbor area."

The *Restless* was a 265-ton vessel, 108 feet 8 inches in length, 27 feet 8-inch beam. She carried "four 32-pounders, one 20-pounder, a Parrot rifle, four 32-pounders and two heavy 12-pounders." Attached to her was the tender *Two Sisters,* with acting Master R. Chatfield on duty to cruise these waters.[5]

Nevertheless, Confederates of the interior continued to build small boats around bales of cotton and sail them downstream to Carlos Bay evading the Federal blockade. From the Bay they slipped through inside waters of ancient Caloosa down coast and across Florida Bay to Nassau, in the Bahama Islands. There they traded cotton for needed supplies and brought them back the way they had come—in the night.

McKay and Summerlin also made several more runs before the war ended. They evaded the blockade ships by moving their landing places and notifying settlers by word of mouth where to meet them.

During and after the war, yellow fever had taken heavy toll of lives among Union soldiers at Key West as well as of Southern prisoners of war at the "infamous" Federal Prison on Dry Tortugas. The treatment was castor oil. The quantity of castor oil needed was enormous, which created great demand for castor beans.

39

So up from Key West in 1868 to these islands came an ex-Union soldier named William Smith Allen.[6] His big sloop loaded with tools and workers, Allen landed on Ybel, cleared what was needed of land and set out fields of castor beans. When his crop flourished, he cleared more land and planted more beans.

The ripe castor beans were transported by schooner to Key West where they were pressed to extract the oil in a special plant. Allen did so well that in 1873 a Mr. Harris came up from Key West and set out a fine crop of his own castor beans.

The men met with disaster that year when a hurricane brought higher than usual tides. Salt water destroyed the bean crops and the equipment. The "farmers" salvaged what they could and returned to Key West.

About the time Allen had arrived on Sanibel, U.S. Deputy Engineer Captain Clay surveyed Punta Rassa across the Bay. Events that followed eventually brought a light house to Sanibel. Meanwhile the Inter-Ocean Telegraph Company of Newark, New Jersey,[7] claimed the barracks and buildings of old Fort Dulaney. It soon had telegraph lines strung on poles through Florida—and, via Punta Rassa, under the waters to Key West and Havana, Cuba.

In 1870 Jake Summerlin received an unlimited order for beef cattle from the Spanish government. He began building the Summerlin House (later called Towle's House) at the old Port of Carlos. In the surrounding cattle pens there, gaudily dressed Spaniards, riding fine horses with *muy importante-mente,* cantered into the cattle pens and selected wild longhorns for purchase.

The Cuban cattle ships sometimes arrived at night. Sanibel and the islands jutted out into the Gulf as they had when Ponce came seeking his fortune centuries before. Point Ybel still could not be seen in the dark so ships had to be piloted in by instinct and long experience to anchor in Carlos Bay.

Even so, it was to be many years before the Sanibel Light House would be erected, for government ways were devious and slow and the islands were far away.

Two early views of Sanibel Island Light Station. There was about a quarter of a mile of sandy shore between the Light House and the Bay of Carlos then and there were many trees, buttonwood, mangroves and sea grapes, and groves of sabal palms.—U.S. Coast Guard Photo National Archives

Chapter 7

The Light House and Point Ybel . . .

Demands for a light house at Point Ybel began to be requested as early as December 10, 1856. Twenty-one years later, a Light House district engineer surveyed the forty-two acres referred to in a plat of December 21, 1877, and asked that action be taken by the secretary of the U.S. Treasury to obtain title to "land requested in 1856."[1]

After almost endless correspondence between numerous

41

governmental agencies, twenty-five years after the first request was made, an act of Congress (1881) authorized the erection of a Sanibel Light House.

But in 1882, a memorandum came to light stating that islands requested in "the 1877 data" had all been withdrawn for Light House purposes by letter from the General Land Office.

Another year went by. April 5, 1883, the Light House engineer from New Orleans surveyed Sanibel and a tract of land (forty-two acres), embracing all of the end of the island east of longitude 82° 01' west from Greenwich, was reserved.

Then, on April 20, Vice Admiral S. C. Rowan requested that "more land than necessary be secured . . ." and the Light House Board requested a permanent reservation of certain lots containing 667.92 acres to "allow for later erosion."[2]

Then, another problem arose. It was learned that the land did not belong to the United States at all. It had presumably been given to Florida under the Swamp Lands Act of 1850. So, the Department of the Interior wrote to the governor of Florida and requested that the state relinquish claim to Sanibel.[3]

"We plan to let a contract within a few days to construct a light-house thereon," said the letter, ". . . viz Fractional Sections 20, 21 and 29, Twp. 46 S., R 23 E, lying in the County of Monroe. . . . These described tracts, also claimed by Florida as Swamp Lands, having been selected and reported to this office as such August 2, 1877. But they have not been approved or patented to the State. . . . In view of these facts, request Florida relinquish to U.S. any and all claims . . . to said lands under the Swamp Land Grant of September 28, 1850."

Governor W. D. Bloxham promptly sent forward his official statement giving up state claims to Sanibel;[4] and the Light House building was commenced.

A contract was executed August 29, 1883, with the Phoenix Iron Company to furnish metal work for the Light House, and in recent news reports it has often been said that the Light was completed in 1884. Even some official records verify this, yet others disagree.

During the many years Henry Shanahan was Keeper of the Light, children (there were thirteen of them) would walk home from school and remain for the fun that was there. In time they danced to Mr. Edison's phonograph; sometimes there were guitars or a fiddle.

Little children found seashells and wonder on the shore. There were wild birds and deer. Above is the Keeper's pet deer, with Roland Shanahan and Grinnel Shanahan (named for Admiral Grinnel, whose ship was captained by Leonard Santini). The deer would run up and down after the Keeper, so he had to build a fence to keep it out of the Light House.—Photo from Clarence Rutland

Light House, Sanibel Island, Fla.

Above: The government wharf that served the Light House and dwellings about 1900 was 168 feet out in the bay, with a boathouse at the shore end and a T-head at the outer end where the channel ran close on its way to the Gulf. The boathouse was connected with the wharf by a platform and had steps leading down to the water.—Photo courtesy Louise Waldron

43

The following, taken from a "Report of the Light House Board, 1884," headed "Sanibel Island, Punta Rassa Harbor, Fla.," explains the confusion in a surprising way:[5]

"Work upon this station was commenced in February when a wharf, 162 feet long, with a T-head 30 by 60 feet, was built upon creosoted piles.

"Material for the dwellings and the foundation of the tower was landed. The dwellings are nearly finished and the foundation for the tower completed.

"The iron work for the tower . . . was shipped from Jersey City, and, when within about two miles of the wharf at Sanibel Island, the schooner having this iron work on board was wrecked.

"A part of the cargo was put on shore, and the balance was abandoned with the wreck by the master of the wrecked schooner.

"The L. H. Engineer, with the crews and working party from the tenders *Arbutus* and *Mignonette* and a diver, afterwards fished up all of the wrecked iron, and landed it on the wharf at Sanibel Island, with the exception of two small gallery brackets, duplicates of which were afterwards made in New Orleans. Owing to this delay the station will not be completed until some time in August."

It is interesting to note here that the ancient island point was still called "Ybel" in most Light House Board documents. Sometimes it was referred to as ". . . the southeast end of Sanibel Island, eastern entrance to Charlotte Harbor." Again, a Coast Survey Chart of 1883 "for Light House purposes," referred to it as "Caloosa Entrance, Fla." A U.S. Coast Guard map of 1884 listed it as: "Sanibel Island Light Station, Punta Rassa Harbor, Fla." The next year, headed "Sanibel Island, entrance to San Carlos Harbor and Port of Punta Rassa, Florida," gave details of the completed new Light Station:

"This structure was commenced in March 1884, and on August 20, 1885, was completed and lighted for the first time.[6]

"The tower is a skeleton iron structure, in general shape that of a frustum of a four-sided pyramid, having a central

44

circular cylinder inclosing a spiral stairway for reaching the lantern. The cylinder does not reach the base of the pyramid, but starts from the top of an iron column, thoroughly braced, 20 feet above the ground.

"The whole is surmounted by an iron watch-room and a lantern, each having a separate gallery and railing. The light is 98 feet above sea level.

"At a short distance from the tower, and connected with it by a stairway, are two detached frame dwellings, resting on well-braced iron columns. . . .

"The lens is of the third order, and the light is fixed, varied by white flashes. . . ."

Dudley Richardson was appointed acting L.H. keeper,[7] August 16, 1884 (the date the Light was to begin operating but did not), and John Johnson, was acting assistant keeper.

The first permanent L.H. keeper was Henry Shanahan. His assistant was Eugene H. Shanahan. They received $740 and $600 per annum, respectively.

The first Sanibel Light was a coal-oil burner with a big, long mantle. The keeper had to climb up and light it with a match at sundown and put it out at dawn. It was operated by a contraption like a clock by a weight on a rope which was synchronized with the flashing light, and had to be "wound up" at regular intervals. A board was laid across inside the tower to hold the weight at sunrise when the light was put out, and left so until time to start it up again.

The kerosene fuel, in five-gallon cans, was carried up the spiral stairway a few steps at a time; in the narrow confines of the tower, this was quite an ordeal.

When not on duty, the keeper and assistant keeper were kept busy with constant painting, cleaning, and repairing something or another pertaining to the Light House, its buildings, and the grounds.

The Light House keepers lived in the two houses at the base of the tower, for Henry had fetched his family up from Key West and there was plenty of room for all. There were only five families on the sprawling island then and they lived out of sight and around the Bay and elsewhere. But the Shan-

Above: Notice the high steps leading up to the dwellings and the higher steps leading up to the tower that led to the light. All important buildings were raised on piles and thoroughly braced to guard against possible damage from high storm tides. The Keeper had to lug drums of kerosene up those steps and up the tower to keep the light burning in the earliest days.—U.S. Coast Guard Photo National Archives

ahans did not mind, they lived happily at Point Ybel for years.

Henry had been a seaman and skillful ship's carpenter. He saw that the Light House and the dwelling houses were scrubbed down continuously. Even the steps leading down to the sandy shore were scrupulously cleaned and painted.

He also had a fine garden patch, including unusually excellent pumpkins. Some years when they ripened under the hot sun, it made the ancient Point Ybel a picture of golden orange pumpkins and vivid green foliage among the white sands and the sea.

Not only did the Light House warn ships at sea of danger; it became a comforting place, a joyous place, and a refuge as the decades came and went.

The keeper had seven children and when his wife died, there they were, motherless young, the nearest house a considerable distance away at the edge of the L.H. Reservation (beyond where the Standard Oil station is today, where Bailey's Road runs down to the Bay).

46

That was the home of the Rutlands, who had arrived from Lake Apopka. After a while, old man Rutland died and left his widow, Irene, with five little ones to care for—a frightening and lonely life.

So, directly Henry married Irene. His children welcomed her children to the Light House point and after a while Henry and Irene had a child of their own.

Altogether, there were thirteen young folks and as they grew there was always something going on around old Point Ybel.

Henry, in his spare time, made adorable models of the Light House keepers' cottages—large enough for the smaller children to play house in. The replicas were perfect in all details and were a joy to his family and all children who came visiting in later years, until a storm washed them away.

He had a trained cat that went about with him constantly. It would roll over like a trained dog at his command. In time when there was a milk cow for the expanded family, the cat learned to sit up and catch a stream of milk direct from the cow's udder when it was turned her way, which pleased the young immensely.

Sometimes the youngsters were privileged to climb the ninety-eight steps of the tall column to the light, counting them as they climbed with Henry. The stair spiral was very narrow, with only inches on either side of Henry or his assistant when they climbed up with the oil drums or to clean the light, and the children could hardly see out of the little windows that marked the rest places for Henry along the way upward.

In hurricane time, Cubans from Havana, and elsewhere in that country, came in their vessels to Carlos Bay off Point Ybel Light. In their schooners known as "fishing smacks," they fished on the snapper and grouper banks off the coast of southwest Florida and were licensed by the captain general of Cuba—as they had been for centuries.

Each fishing smack had a well inside which let water in from below up to a certain depth. In these wells, the fish catches were "stored" and kept alive, without ice, until they could be delivered to the markets of Cuba.

Even in a hurricane, the Light House knew laughter and song. Above is a Cuban fishing smack that in 1947 was blown from Carlos Bay all the way to Cape Romano. Then, when the wind turned, it was blown back over almost the same course, and foundered and broke up on the bar near the Sanibel Light.

One Cuban drowned; one was located on Pine Island and brought to the Light House. Two seamen and one goat, with its feet still tied together, landed on Captiva.

Islanders gathered clothing for the men and some of the garbs were a curious sight. The cabin boy was particularly ludicrous in a man's sweat shirt that flopped about him whenever he tried to navigate. They were fed and sheltered at the Light House until they could be returned to their native land.

Nowadays (since Castro took over Cuba), after centuries of sailing into Carlos Bay for refuge in storm, the Cuban fishing smacks come to Sanibel no more.— Sketch by Eleanor D. Clapp

Fishing smacks carried barometers and fishermen knew when a bad storm or hurricane was approaching. At such times, they would head for Point Ybel and lie to behind the islands until the storm was over.

During later farming years on Sanibel, Cubans would slip ashore and trade *aguardiente* (Cuban rum) to field workers for delicious tomatoes that were growing in the fields. Northern tourists who occasionally visited the islands then were afraid when they saw Cubans roaming the shore—perhaps because the sailors carried knives (necessities of life for men of the sea); perhaps they were stirred by the vague tales of reckless pirates that still were being told in gory detail.

Earliest island dwellers around the Light House remembered otherwise.

One day, Cubans ashore stopped at one of the dwellings at Point Ybel and gesticulated in many ways around their heads, indicating they wanted something, but what? *"No sabe,"* they were told.

Then one brightened. He drew an excellent picture of a pair of scissors, and the others understood: The Cubans wanted to borrow a pair of scissors with which to cut the hair of the men of the fishing smacks. They accepted the scissors and departed.

Later, when they returned with the scissors, they also brought a big, freshly caught fish as a gift of appreciation. They gesticulated for paper and laid it on the porch outdoors. They laid the fish there and deftly filleted it, then rolled up all the mess and carried it away with them, calling *"muchus gracios,"* as they went their way.

Another time, during a hurricane, a crew of the Cubans came ashore and sought refuge in the Light House for the duration. The wife of the keeper was pregnant and the Cubans, respectful of motherhood-to-be, solicitously took over.

They placed her in a chair and commenced operations on their own. They cooked for all, washed dishes, and—true to the habits of the sea—scrubbed the kitchen after each meal was finished.

One other small episode is well remembered. In those days you could walk out on the beach in front of the Light House. Out there was the garden, and the privies, one of which was on the shore facing the sea.

When the expected hurricane had gone and the Cubans presumably gone, the expectant mother went out to the privy on the shore. Leaving the door open, she blissfully was watching the far horizons.

But as she sat comfortably on her throne, along the shore came four of the Cuban sailors, for they had not yet sailed away. Alarmed and embarrassed, she sat there wondering what to do. The lads, suddenly aware of the situation, nevertheless came onward.

When the lead sailor was opposite her on the shore, he bowed very low from his waist, as one would to a queen, and passed soberly on. Following his lead, bowing from the waist, each of the others passed and went sturdily on, as if he had had audience with royalty.

Where else would so appropriate a way of handling so awkward a situation happen except on this island in the sea?

In later years small steamers came, churning their way from island to island, bringing baseball players, picnic parties, and shell gatherers on holiday from upriver to Point Ybel.

But all of this—the Light House and dwellings, the many children, the gentle sailors, picnics and baseball—were to become part of the lore of the islands.

Part II

OF HOMESTEADERS AND STEAMBOATS

Chapter 8

Woodring Point and Tarpon Bay . . .

The islands were never quite deserted. In 1869, Adolphus Santini was living on Sanibel. He soon moved on downcoast to the shell mounds of Chokoloskee Island. The U.S. Census of 1870,[1] under a heading "Sinnabel Island, Monroe County," listed residents of Sanibel as:

Wm. S. Allen, Asst. Marshall of Monroe County, and wife.
George W. Allen, age 16.

In that Census, there was no mention of Captiva Island. Cayo Costa, north of Captiva, was spelled "Cayo Acosta, Charlotte Harbor,"[2] and inhabitants were enumerated as follows:

Philipe Santini, 66, farmer, Italy
Mary Santini, 50, France
Adolphus Santini, 30, farmer, Louisiana
Irene Santini, 26, housekeeper, Georgia
Mary P. Santini, 21, Florida
Nicholas Santini, 27, farmer, Florida
Dorinela Santini, 21, housekeeper, Florida
Angela Santini, 18, housekeeper, Florida

The Census taker seems to have ignored Indians and Spanish Indians, of whom only a few were left.

The islands were not unnoticed, however. Boston promoters developed a "high flying dream" of building a modern city on the tip of Pine Island, across from Sanibel, in 1885. They set out coconut palms and dreamed of pleasant leisure there despite the mosquitoes, high tides, and wilderness surroundings.

They named their place "Saint-James-City-on-the-Gulf."

53

They advertised in advance, then started building a dock, a supply store and a rambling, big frame hotel (see sketch on page 79). The grandiose scheme only lasted five years, yet it brought the Woodrings to Sanibel.

Sam C. Woodring, Sr., of Hazelton, Pennsylvania, read the advertisements. He had been in Key West during the recent war and remembered the islands. After the war he had rambled about, married, and roamed some more. Being a blacksmith by trade, he could always find work. So, Sam with his wife, Anna, and son, Sam, Jr., age nine, moved to Saint-James-City-on-the-Gulf. Mrs. Woodring operated a "boarding-house" for the workers who were building the city-to-be.

In the store by the Bay, one day, Sam met another Sam, Captain Sam Ellis, who turned out to be a boisterous, ex-British Navy man, living in solitude on Sanibel.

The Britisher regaled Woodring with tales of lovely Ellis Bay and the shell mounds of the ancient Indians high above the waters, where a man did not have to work, just sail a little boat around and enjoy leisurely living.

In a short time, Sam Woodring and his family had moved over to Sanibel and settled on a bay at the place now known as "Woodring Point." The splendid shell mounds along the bay have long since been hauled away, Ellis Bay had become Tarpon Bay, but the Woodring place still stands.

Sam Woodring had lumber sent up from Key West by schooner with which to build the two-story frame house fronting the Bay. Furniture came the same way. Red mangroves, standing on weird arching bases with interlacing branches, formed an almost impenetrable jungle around it on the landward side. Gumbo-limbo trees reached from the shell mounds up into the far blue sky. In time, the Woodrings had date palms growing there.

The first white child was born on Sanibel, April 25, 1888, to Sam and Anna Woodring. She was named Flora Sanibel Woodring.

The Woodrings did not have much of a garden. A few greens and some sweet yams were raised in the shell-earth. Before Flora had been born her brother, Sam, age nine, had learned to throw a cast net like the Spanish Indians did and

On Carlos Bay, near Tarpon Bay, at what was to become known as Woodring Point, stood the Woodring home in the 1880's. It was built of lumber fetched by schooner from Key West. There, Captain Sam Ellis later married his Indian bride and there early homesteaders often stopped over, when they arrived to establish land claims.

Left to right are: George Underhill, Allie Collins, Carl Woodring, Mrs. Samuel C. (Anna) Woodring, Sr., Annie Woodring, Sam Woodring, Jr., Samuel Woodring, Sr., and Mr. Gooddell. The children are Flora, first white child born on Sanibel and her small brother, Harrison Woodring.—Photo courtesy Flora Morris

he easily caught all the fish the family wanted from the little dock out in front. He had learned to turn over rocks and find delicious stone crabs, gathered coon oysters from among the mangroves and clams from the clam beds offshore.

Old Sam (who was not so old then but who died when Flora was only ten years old) built a smokehouse. There he used buttonwood for fuel and smoked victuals. He sun dried food, too, spreading it out on sunny days to the sun and air, keeping them dry in the smokehouse at other times.

In her island kitchen, Sam's wife, Anna, used large iron, stone, or china bowls for a good deal of her cookery. She had much tinware, copper dishpans, pie pans, and the like. Since fresh water was scarce, barrels covered with cheesecloth, were set out to catch rainwater. Later there would be a cistern.

Fuel for the wood-burning stove was cut from nearby button-wood hammocks.

On this subtropical island in the sun there was then an amazing variety of food and many ways of cooking it.

Anna Woodring sometimes pickled fish. She would put a little lard, vinegar, and seasonings into an iron pot, cut mullet into pieces or fillets, and add them to the vinegar with bay leaves and whole cloves and let them cure.

She would slice turtle meat or cut it into chunks and salt it down in crocks. Turtle meat kept covered with brine was "pickled." It could be removed as needed and covered with water overnight to remove the salt. Then it was "as good as fresh meat."

Perhaps unknown to the Woodrings, almost a hundred years before their time and for thousands of years prior to that, Indians then Spanish-Indians had been pickling and sun drying mullet roe and black drum roe. After the pickling and sun drying, such roes were pressed between two boards and "exposed upon a hurdle in a shallow hut to the smoak of the inner part of the ears of corn, which is properly the receptacle of the seed and called cobs. These roes, the Spaniards are very fond of and use them instead of cavear. . . ."[3]

Edible birds were "night squawks," curlews (the pink curlews were best), roseate spoonbills, and gannets (also called ironheads or wood storks). Wild birds were used like chicken is today and were especially delicious fried.

There were land tortoises or Florida gophers living in burrows all over the interior of the islands. These furnished meat that tasted somewhat similar to veal and were used to make "gopher stew with dumplings," a great favorite with men and boys.

One of the best remembered early foods was rabbit meat for wild brown rabbits were astonishingly plentiful on Sanibel. Easily caught, they were skinned and cleaned, salted and peppered, and baked in rows on tin baking sheets until they became a delectable golden brown.

Most of these foods are now outlawed but in those days there was no ice, the steamer only arrived at Saint-James-on-the-Gulf three times weekly and all supplies had to be fetched from there by sail or row boat. So wild food sustained them.

As Sam and his sons came to love the Bay and open seas, the little Woodring girl came to love the white sands of the Gulf front of the island. There were sea grasses and morning glories and sweet sea lavender. She found colorful seashells and small sea treasures among the spindrift. When she was older, she sensed the wonder of these islands and sometimes dug into the Indian mounds, sometimes watched the far horizons of the rolling Gulf—as it had been for thousands of years.

When she had grown old, Flora remembered when the famous archeologist named Cushing had visited Captain Sam Ellis of Tarpon Bay, and when her father had guided him among the ancient shell mounds that still remained. The former she recalled because Cushing later had sent her father a fine bound book about the things he had discovered. The latter she remembered for other reasons.

Although she was only ten years old when it happened, she particularly recalled Captain Sam Ellis when he married. On his wedding day he was roaring drunk, dancing around,

The wide, shell-strewn beach where early homesteaders roamed. This view was a postcard made for and sold by the Sanibel Packing Company, established by the Bailey Brothers in 1899 on the Bay side of the island.

57

having a fine time—grabbing his wife, hugging and kissing her. The "wedding" was held in the Woodring home.

The bride was an Indian girl that the captain had "found" living in the cove beyond Reed's place (for others had come to the islands). She was timid and primitive as she had never been away from the local region.

The newlyweds built a little new palmetto shack among the other palm-thatched shelters on the south shore of Tarpon Bay. Their "home" had an earth floor but "it was kept as clean and neat as could be." Visitors were seated on cowhide seated chairs, but she was gentle and gracious. She made spreads of pieced quilt and presumably made the captain happy.

Flora Woodring remembered her best when she had grown to be a tall, angular woman. Distrusting white men's medicine, she used primitive Indian remedies for illnesses. She was a fine midwife; and she scraped deer horn parts to make a special tea for afterbirth.

In recent years, published items have sometimes romantically reported that Captain Sam Ellis and his wife died and were buried together on Sanibel. Actually, Widow Ellis was married again downcoast and had other children. But that is another of the lost stories of these islands.

Above: The sisters, nucleus of Casa Ybel. It fronted the open Gulf of Mexico and was first named for the two Barnes girls who operated it. The girls' parents had been missionaries to India, so The Sisters served delicious food, using much curry and other spices, augmented by Kentucky cooking. Guests relished it and came back year after year for more.

Gradually, cabins were built around the original building and called "guest cottages." The imaginative Barnes family re-named their white-washed settlement "Casa Ybel" which, they said, meant "The House of Isabella."

Below: Copy of an advertisement of the early Casa Ybel, about 1909.—Old Fort Myers Press Photo

60

Chapter 9

Early settlers on Gulf front and Bay . . .

The Sanibel Light had been operating three years before the island was opened to homesteading by the government. The entire end of Sanibel from Point Ybel to what is now Bailey's Road, from Carlos Bay to the Gulf, belonged to the Light House; and homesteaders and other settlers, therefore, settled along the Gulf shore for pleasure, along the Bay for transportation, and other places for later farming.

One of the first homesteaders was George Barnes and his wife, who became known later as "Mama Barnes." Both were tall and lean. George and his wife had been members of various religious denominations. They had started out from Louisville, Kentucky, and as a mountain evangelist, George had served as a missionary in India for years.

George believed that God would take care of him and somehow God did. The one girl sang alto, the other soprano, and the missionary carried along a small melodeon as well as a Bible and the family roamed from Calcutta to Bombay, as they tried to elevate the "heathen."

When George Barnes decided he could no longer preach in foreign lands (about 1882), he wandered into Florida, U.S.A. Eventually, Barnes reached Punta Gorda and heard of the homestead opportunity on Sanibel. Without ado, he fetched his family southward.

Barnes and wife, his two daughters and son homesteaded— some say 160 acres, some say that many each. They built "The Sisters" on the Gulf and the Misses Mary and Georgia Barnes "accepted guests" there, the only such place on the Gulf front for some years.

Perhaps the most remarkable early family, and the one that left the most lasting impression on the islands, was that of Laetitia Lafon Ashmore Nutt.

She was born in Woodford County, Kentucky, in 1836. She married Captain L. M. Nutt, a lawyer and later a senator from Caddo Parish, Louisiana. Throughout the War Between the States (Civil War), Laetitia followed her beloved husband from one battlefield to another and kept a diary from day to day which is still extant.

At Ringgold, Georgia, she and her two sisters were almost made prisoners of war. The Federals had already taken possession of Ringgold when Major John Young Rankin, of the Twenty-fifth Texas Cavalry, with a small body of men, volunteered to try to rescue them from the outskirts where they were waiting.

The girls were given three minutes to prepare themselves and join the troopers. They hastily were mounted, each behind one of the men, and all set out full speed to escape. The alarmed Northern pickets came after, in full pursuit. At intervals, Rankin and some of his men stopped to exchange shots and hold back their pursuers, then rode on with the girls again, until at last they found safety behind the Confederate lines.

Laetitia's love story for her husband became legendary; and the Louisville, Kentucky, *Democrat,* in 1883, paid glowing tribute to her and her daughters.

So Laetitia came in sorrow and to "create a new home" on Sanibel with her daughters, Letitia, Cordelia, and Nanny, and her brother, James Keith Ashmore.

Sustained by their memories, she and her family adjusted to the wilderness of sea and sky among the sabal palms and sea grapes. They built Gray Gables high above the ground to escape hurricane tides. Kitchen and dining room were below, as was the custom in old Southern homes from where they had come, and the living quarters were above. (The original bay window still looks out over the sunlit sea.)

A low ancient shell ridge protected the Gables from the Gulf but once you climbed it, you could see white sands,

Above: The Nutt girls and their pet dog, with Laetitia Nutt half-hidden in the shadows, at Gray Gables about 1889. To Sanibel they brought past gentility and small treasures such as daguerreotypes of worthy kindred and Confederate flags their loved ones had served so well. On one wall they spread the illustrious genealogy of their family to remind them of proud yesterdays.—Photo courtesy Eleanor Pearse Estate

Below: Gray Gables today. Inside there are still scrapbooks of poetry, essays, and clippings; heirlooms; Confederate flags; the amazing "family tree" on the wall. Here the Confederate widow and her daughters lived out their lives, and bequeathed to early islanders knowledge and culture because they came long ago.

The bay window of the old home (above) is still part of the expanded home shown here, owned by descendants today.—Photo courtesy Florence Martin

63

The Matthews, fronting the Gulf of Mexico. These cottages were built after the early wharves had been erected on Carlos Bay and the Gulf. In time, The Matthews was composed of numerous cottages, all nicely furnished, with large parlors for dancing, commodious dining rooms, and verandas on all buildings. Delicious foods were served, Southern style. Negro help came from Georgia each winter to work and live on the premises; they sang as they worked, adding an easygoing South Seas atmosphere.

Both Casa Ybel and The Matthews offered separate "bath houses" on the white sandy shore for ladies and gentlemen. The Matthews had a pier, with a small pavilion on the end, extending out into the Gulf.—Photo from old Fort Myers Press 1909

foam-flecked waters, and the far horizon from among palms and whispering pines and there was strange peace.

From Gray Gables, Laetitia and her daughters ever after went forth to teach school, to tend the post office, and to wield cultural influence over the newly populated islands. Of all the family (widowed Laetitia, Miss Cordie, and Miss Letitia) only Miss Nannie married and that was late in life—to a Mr. Holt.

When the W. J. Matthews family came in 1895, his father, Lucien, also spent the winter at "The Sisters." Lucien returned north. The Matthewses remained and built an "eight room, nicely furnished home with broad verandas," on the Gulf near the Jane Matthews wharf.

Later, they followed the Barnes' pattern and began to "accept guests." It is remembered that Mr. Matthews was a "bril-

64

liant man," who tried to farm and helped around the hotel. Mrs. Matthews—in later years called "Granny" Matthews—lived to be ninety-four years old and beloved by all along the Gulf.

The few early tourists that came to Sanibel arrived by steamer and reached Casa Ybel and The Matthews over a sandy trail from the landing, known as the Tarpon Bay Road. A high-built, two-wheeled cart, drawn by a mule, fetched trunks and boxes from the steamer landing and tourists often walked the mile and a half to Casa Ybel.

Heat, flies, and mosquitoes plagued travelers. There were small alligators in the roadside ditches and larger ones in the marshes. Occasionally, a big alligator, sunning itself, would rise suddenly and crawl across the road: The vehicle and travelers had to halt until the creature vanished into the watery grasses on the other side.

Along the Gulf between the Barnes, Matthews, and Nutt dwellings there was a unique sort of culture that grew pleasantly over the years. *Scribner's* and *Harper's* magazines came via steamer and were read. Cards were played. There was dancing.

The Matthews children went up the Gulf shore to the Nutt girls' home for instruction, or the Nutt girls came and taught them at The Matthews. Other times, the children went to a public school in the old Fitzhugh house.

All the Barneses could speak and sing well. Tall, lean "Mama" Barnes would read to the Matthews children. Tall, lean, ex-missionary George Barnes would make candy and tell them stories. The Barneses' three grandchildren later played with the Matthews children.

They all seemed somehow young and gay as they visited each other, to and fro, along the road by the Gulf. Once, George Barnes put the melodeon on a wagon and hauled it along the shore to The Matthews where they played Christmas carols and sang joyously together by the sea.

How did outsiders know about Sanibel? George Barnes made an ambitious trip up through Kentucky telling of the wonders of the island, and The Sisters, or Casa Ybel, grew beyond its capacity.

Meanwhile, Georgia Barnes married a Major Edward Duncan. It was he who was most obliging and willing to help out, even with cooking at The Sisters when necessary.

The Duncans built a two-story rococo house that had curious cupolas and porches which they named "Thistle Lodge." They also erected a little church for George Barnes.

Over on the Bay side of the island, a Captain W. H. Reed and son, William, age twenty-one, had come. They were from Portland, Maine, and were acquainted with the Maine folks across on the end of Pine Island. Like Barnes, Reed had been at the end of the railroad in 1887, at Punta Gorda, and heard of the proposed homesteading of Sanibel.

In 1888, Captain Reed and his son arrived. They settled on Carlos Bay. As homesteaders began farming, Reed bought first one boat then others to carry the produce away. Young Sam Woodring, of Woodring Point, captained one of Reed's boats.

Other homesteaders arriving about that time were the Reverend George Fitzhugh and family from Virginia, George Bullock, and a man named Wirene and family. Some of these

The curious "rococo" style E. M. Duncan home on the Gulf which they called "Thistle Lodge." Mrs. Duncan had been Georgia Barnes, daughter of the Missionary Barnes family who homesteaded land and operated The Sisters that later became Casa Ybel.—Old Press photo, 1903

66

were said to have landed in a sailboat with Captain Montgomery. E. T. Pell came also.

There came to be many island worlds but the incoming homesteaders paid little attention to any but their own.

It was said that some who sailed these waters were smuggling *aguardiente,* a potent rum, in large narrow-necked bottles of glass or stoneware—because that was more profitable than fishing.

One newspaper of that day reported that "a number of persons over in Charlotte Harbor had complaints made against them for handling smuggled China rum. . . ."

A few years later, the *New York World* printed an account of the capture of a Spanish smuggling vessel. It said: "Several families live on Sanibel Island, and those adjacent, who are supposed to be aiders and abettors in the smuggling business."

Quaint church built for George Barnes, once missionary to India, by his daughter and son-in-law, the Duncans. It stood about where Mrs. Perry, of Asheville, had her home, Spindrift, many years later and was "next door" to what was then the island cemetery, which Barnes had set aside for future contingencies.

There, a cross rose high in the sky, which Barnes hoped would attract and somehow encourage seamen sailing down coast offshore. Some islanders say the church blew away in a hurricane; others say some of its salvaged timbers and lumber are part of one of the Casa Ybel cottages still.—Sketch from old photo by Eleanor D. Clapp

The article writer wondered slyly if Reverends Fitzhugh, Barnes, and Dunlop had not better "move, or institute a suit for libel."

The earliest settlers of Sanibel were predominantly Southern. A few came from Maine, one from Pennsylvania; there was a German and Canadian on Captiva, an Austrian on Buck Key, and Spaniards or Spanish Indians in remote areas, fishing. Otherwise, they were descendants of early American pioneers and the majority had been impoverished for decades following the War Between the States.

They came from Kentucky, Virginia, Georgia, Louisiana, upper Florida, and other old Confederate states. All of them became "characters" or rather "individuals" and taken as a whole, they made the early islands what they eventually became: easy-going hideaways of happiness for all who came.

None expected to become rich in this world's goods, but they became rich in day-to-day little joys.

There are many island legends about this old Breckinridge House. Presumably it was first built by Elbert Willis, about 1899. The land on which it stood had been owned by one family since it was homesteaded under President Benjamin Harrison in 1891 until 1955, through inheritance by aunts, cousins, and others.

It stood in the vicinity of the Barnes, Matthews and Nutt homes; but, unlike Casa Ybel, Gray Gables and The Matthews, this place suffered hurricane and fire. It was always rebuilt, however. Today the site is occupied by the famed Hurricane House, owned by the Paul and Richard Kearns families. They purchased it from the last of the old family line.—Photo courtesy Hurricane House and the Kearns families

68

Chapter 10

Pine Island Sound and Carlos Bay . . .

Sanibel and Captiva did not have adequate docking facilities at first. There were only sailing vessels anchored offshore, and for a time the *Alice Howard,* captained by William White, sailed three times weekly down Pine Island Sound through Carlos Bay and up the Caloosa Hatchee to Myers, Florida. It stopped at tiny Saint-James-City-on-the-Gulf and at remote Punta Rassa on its way.

The H. B. Plant Railroad penetrated south to Punta Gorda, *circa* 1887, and refused to come farther, but it did put on a railroad owned steamer.[1]

This big steamer could not get near the islands, except at the Light House wharf. So the early settlers received mail, food, and supplies—not available in natural state on the islands or in the waters—over at Saint James. The big steamer put cargo and passengers off on the dock there and settlers had to sail or row across the Bay to get them.

Later, when long docks had been built from the shore of Sanibel out to the deep water channel, two steamers were put on this run and there was daily service to the islands.

There were fine state-rooms on board, for these were all-day trips. There was rich color, carpeting, a dining room with excellent food—a splendid salon, enjoyed by newcomers and islanders who sailed these waters.

Out of the morning mists up Punta Gorda way, the steamer would sail majestically on its way, smoke from her stacks rising in the still air.

As she came down Pine Island Sound, she would blow her whistle when still a quarter of a mile away—three long

69

blasts—to warn islanders to come to the docks. And eager folks bestirred themselves with cries of "Here she comes!"

The captain had a bell with which he instructed the engineer below how and when to back and maneuver to the dock. The captain held the handle of a wire in his hand that pulled the signal bell below. When he wanted the steamer to go ahead, he pulled once; to reverse, he pulled twice.

The white captain had two mates. There was once a one-eyed Negro helmsman who helped steer one of the steamers. On long runs he would relieve the captain but give the helm back as they approached a new landing, for the captain was responsible for the ship. The firemen below were sometimes white, sometimes Negro.

When horses, mules (and sometimes a cow) were destined

South from Point Ybel most coastal islands were uninhabited except for itinerant coastal people; so it was northward. Up the Caloosa Hatchee and south by east deep in the Everglades Indians still poled their canoes and built their campfires amid their palm-thatched cheekees. Now and then a schooner brought a cargo of stag or brain coral up from the Caribbean. Sometimes they were suspected of smuggling in rum.—Photo from old Press 1903

70

for the islands, they were quartered toward the back of the deck in fenced off pens.

At the steamer landings, Negro deckhands handled freight and lines as the big boat eased in to the wharf. There was singing and laughter and good-natured rivalry as the cargoes were loaded and unloaded.

Always there was an air of expectant excitement around the docks, nearly always a cluster of settlers was there. Sometimes an incoming passenger or a newcomer got off, and was met by a wagon or surrey and driven to one of the two "resorts" over on the Gulf side.

The necessity for a dock out to deep water where the steamers could land was obvious almost at once to these Sanibel settlers.

On January 20, 1890, Mrs. Laetitia Nutt, postmaster,[2] requested that the wife of the assistant light house keeper be

Another view of the *St. Lucie*, with Captain H. Fisher, coming down Pine Island Sound to Carlos Bay. The ship had twenty-four state-rooms because the run took all day. As homesteaders came and farming progressed, the *Thomas A. Edison*, with Captain Nick Armeda, was added to the run.—Old Press photo 1903

allowed to "act as postmistress" until a landing pier could be built elsewhere.

A month later, she asked permission to have mail and freight landed "on the government wharf at the Light House," until a pier could be built.

On March 11, she asked permission to erect a pier and post office on the Light House Reservation because there was no other "suitable site." At the same time, she asked permission be granted for palms to be cut on the reservation for pilings for the pier.

The L.H. Board said such permission would be contingent on a plat of the location being presented. No palms were to be cut.

Reverend Mr. Barnes addressed the L.H. Board April 9, 1890,[3] stating that the L.H. inspector had forbidden the steamer to land at the L.H. Wharf, causing the settlers great hardship. Barnes asked permission for the steamer to land. June 19, the L.H. inspector recommended that mail, passengers, and light freight be allowed to land at the L.H. Wharf until the settlers could build their pier.

Next Reverend Mr. Fitzhugh wrote the L.H. Board for permission to build a wharf at the western part of the L.H. Reservation about a mile and a half from Point Ybel, approximately where Bailey's Road now meets Carlos Bay. A few days later he added a request to build a storehouse near said wharf.

Months later (January 21, 1891), Fitzhugh wrote for a reply[4] to his requests, and March 5, 1892, the L.H. Board granted both. There is no further record of these projects by Fitzhugh.

During this period, two interesting items should be inserted: The first is that from the steamers Sanibel appeared to be without houses—just a lonely island; the second that in 1892 the ancient shell mounds of Sanibel were being loaded onto scows and towed upriver to an old wooden pier, to become "paving material" for roadways around the village of "Myers."[5]

In the village paper that year there was information that "occasionally a Revenue Cutter passes Sanibel in pursuit of

72

Dotted line indicates the railroad steamer route from Punta Gorda down Charlotte Harbor and Pine Island Sound, through Carlos Bay and up the Caloosa Hatchee to Fort Myers.

Early steamer stops were at Saint-James-City-on-the-Gulf and the Light House wharf; later at The Matthews and Reed wharves; and eventually at the Wulfert and Captiva bulkheads.

73

A water spout off Point Ybel and Sanibel Light, entrance of Carlos Bay. The steamer, left, had just left the Matthews wharf but the weather was so rough it returned and tied up to the wharf until the squall passed before crossing the open bay.

On clear days, dolphins rolled and fish abounded in the waters. Heads of great turtles, coming up for air, would dot the surface of the sea.—Photo loaned by Clarence Rutland

some luckless smuggler.[6] Last year a large schooner anchored offshore. In a short time a Revenue Cutter came up and captured her. Leaving some of the Revenue men aboard, it was presumed, the Cutter proceeded to Punta Rassa either to coal up or for some other purposes, and returned to the schooner the next morning.

"The schooner drew too much water to be carried to Punta Rassa and had to be taken all the way to Key West, with the supposed smuggler swearing a blue streak all the way. At Key West, when the vessel was searched, not a single cigar band or drop of rum could be found. In some manner the smuggler had gotten the goods off during the night and landed it on Sanibel Island."

Despite isolation and smuggling, Sanibel continued to press for a dock on the Light House Reservation end of the island. January 16, 1895, Frank Bailey, who had come to farm, wrote the board requesting permission to build a road, wharf, and warehouse near the "western boundary," allowing the government to use it and to revoke its permit at pleasure. The L.H. Board turned down his request.

The arguments by mail went on.

Then, suddenly, when the L.H. inspector arrived "March 28, 1896," he reported hastily that a road had been built across the Reservation and a Mrs. J. V. Matthews (not the Island Inn Matthews) had built a wharf and warehouse on the northwest section "without authority."[7]

"The wharf," said the report, "is maintained in good condition by the people, the navigators, and shipping associations.

"There is a warehouse on the west side of the wharf and a store with living quarters on the east side, both of which are owned and run by John W. Geraty & Company, who conduct a general merchandise and shipping business."[8]

Mrs. Jane Matthews, it seems, was a rich widow from Peewee Valley, Kentucky, who had come to homestead on Sanibel. Little is known about her except that she was called "Aunt Jane" by some islanders and for a time lived with the W. J. Matthews family. Certainly she favored Sanibel with her generosity.

The Matthews Wharf (completed in 1895) was dedicated in 1896 to islanders' use forever by Jane V. Matthews, a widow and homesteader.

Nobody knows who persuaded her to build it but she did. Since this wharf extended to the channel, steamers could at last bring mail, passengers and supplies direct to the island, and take away cargoes of tomatoes and vegetables.

In this photo logs and coconuts of the islands await the coming of the steamer and unknown men await the pleasant excitement to come.—Photo courtesy Albert Schneider

Later records disclose that the dock she built on Carlos Bay and "another elsewhere on the island" had been dedicated by her, through a deed, for "public use."[9]

The wharf on the Gulf side was a pleasure pier; the one on the Bay of greatest importance to islanders.

The indenture made by Jane Matthews being dated February 22, 1896, on the birthday anniversary of George Washington, may have been a small defiant gesture to governmental red tape that had kept the islanders from having communication by vessel with the outside world.

The spot selected for the dock was said to be "the only place where deep water was obtainable and where land for a road to the balance of Sanibel could be built," on account of a mangrove swamp "that makes eastward at that point."

To trustees James Ashmore, Keats Perry, Ernest Bailey, J. J. Chapman, and Allen O. Reeder, and their heirs or successors, Jane Matthews gave full rights forever to the two docks to be known as "the Matthews docks, one on the north or bay side . . . the other on the Gulf side of the said island, Lee County, State of Florida." These to be held forever "for the benefit of the people of the Island of Sanibel. . . ."

The above named men managed the wharf for about two years. J. W. Geraty had it about two more. And thereafter, Frank P. Bailey and his brother, E. R. Bailey, maintained both wharf and buildings.

Meanwhile, the L.H. Board deeded the strip of land to the people and made the whole project legal, for the "benefit" of the islanders forever.

With the new deep water dock where the big steamers could land, it appeared that communication with the outside world by mail was solved. There were some problems, nevertheless: the first concerns who was the first postmaster, the second about a forgotten post office called "Reed" on the Bay.

Despite the long publicized legend that William S. Reed established the first post office, official records disclose that:

"A fourth-class post office was established at Sanibel, Florida, in Lee County on July 31, 1889. It was discontinued on

Left to right are William S. Reed, his son, William Reed, and children. At extreme right is the early Sanibel post office. Adjoining is the Sanibel House, which has the following interesting legend.

Prior to 1900, there had been a "Floating Palace" (a lighter with a hotel built upon it), owned by Ida Hughes and her son-in-law. Each spring, this Floating Palace was towed over to Boca Grande Pass. There it was anchored, with wealthy Northerners aboard who fished for the mighty fighting fish of that Pass.

In off-season, this sea-going house of joy tied up at Reed's. There cards were played, some gambling went on, and drinking—so it was said.

Mrs. J. B. Daniels operated the Floating Palace for a time. When it sank off Reed's, she had the lumber raised up from the waters and erected the Sanibel House. Early in World War I, several thousand pounds of sheet copper were salvaged from the still submerged bottom of the Floating Palace. Now all signs of copper, the palace and hotel are gone.—Photo from old Press, 1909

February 21, 1895, and had only one Postmaster, Laetitia A. Nutt."[10]

More interesting still, these records show that just prior to the ending of Laetitia's career, William S. Reed had established a post office called "Reed, Florida" (December 21, 1894), with himself as postmaster. On April 1, 1895, the name of Reed, Florida, was officially changed to Sanibel, Florida, with William S. Reed, his son, as postmaster.[11]

Whatever rivalry existed then, if any, has become lost in time. Islanders depended upon mail via steamers by which to order everything they needed that was not made or raised on Sanibel and William S. Reed remained in office for decades.

This new Sanibel post office was first located in the Reed home. Shortly afterward it was moved to an adjoining building which also housed a tiny store. It finally became a separate frame building—on the Bay side of the island about a mile from the new Matthews Wharf.

Descendants of early homesteaders have long had a legend that Sanibel Island had the first rural free delivery service in the United States.

This is almost but not quite true.

"Although the Sanibel route was one of the early RFD routes instituted in the United States," according to U.S. Postal Records, "it was not the first. Rural Free Delivery . . . first suggested in 1891 . . . was not started . . . until October 1, 1896 . . . in West Virginia. Nine months later the

The rambling, frame hotel *San Carlos* at Saint-James-on-the-Gulf, Pine Island, across from Sanibel about 1885. The few people there came from Maine and Canada. Earliest yachtsmen anchored offshore. There was a dock, built on high pilings, there and a store and post office. Earliest Sanibel homesteaders rowed or sailed there for mail and supplies.

Earliest young winter visitors from The Sisters (Casa Ybel) or The Matthews would dress in evening clothes and sail over to dance at the hotel, during the short hey-day of that establishment.

If the wind was right, they arrived at the dock and over the shell roadway from bay to hotel rode in a wagonette. This was a vehicle that had two facing seats along the sides back of a transverse seat in front.

If the wind blew the wrong way or died down, the revelers never reached their rendezvous at all. The homesteaders had no interest in such goings on.—Sketch from photo by Eleanor D. Clapp

service had grown to 82 routes, operating from 43 post offices in twenty-nine of the United States. The Sanibel RFD was one of the early routes, however. . . . It was established April 2, 1900."[12]

The first RFD carrier was Joe G. Dowd, who served until May 31, 1907. Other early carriers were Will Harrison, Newton Rutland, and in later years, Webb Shanahan and O. O. Murphy.

By 1900, the mail sack or sacks were put off the steamer at Reed's Dock and dispatched by carrier to the frame post office. From there, an RFD carrier took most of it via horse and buggy, later by automobile, over the Tarpon Bay Road and along what is now Periwinkle Drive to islanders as far away as the vicinity of the present American Legion Home.

By mail, homesteaders continued to order seeds, food, medicine, clothing, lumber, nails, fertilizer. It was their only communication with the outer world. Their lives depended upon it.

Chapter 11

Sanibel tomatoes, Wulfert, and mosquitoes . . .

"There never were tomatoes like those of Sanibel!" has ever been the cry of the islanders. They were not so large but sweet, with a flavor none ever forgot. Even when picked green to ripen later, they had a savoriness unlike any others, and when allowed to ripen on the plants in the sun they were, indeed, perfection.

Islanders ate Sanibel tomatoes twice a day, enjoying them as people elsewhere enjoyed fruit, and as the fame of them spread northward, islanders who raised them in winter prospered.

Moreover, Sanibel land was free, virgin soil. There were no fences, no stock running loose. Homesteads were taken up from fringes of the L.H. Reservation toward Tarpon Bay and Road, along the Gulf and what is now Periwinkle Drive.

When land began to grow scarce in an area, a newcomer could pick out a goodly patch that suited him, plow it up and farm it—and nobody would ask questions. Homesteaders were glad to let others work their land for thus scrub and wild palms were cleared away.

Scattered settlers pushed on to the place now known as Wulfert, where there was access to Bay and Sound. The name's origin is not known. Captain J. J. Dinkins always insisted that some folks lived in that region prior to the 1894-1895 Freeze but he did not know the origin of Wulfert. About 1900, Eleanor Pearse, a winter visitor, wrote "there is a new landing on Sanibel called 'Wulfert.' "[1]

It is possible that people had been living there prior to that

Artist's sketch of early farm scene.—By Eleanor Douglas Clapp

and that farming would by that time support a wharf or landing.

Most old homesteaders say Mason C. Dwight settled Wulfert and that he told them he had named it for the place from whence he had come. Research shows no such place in the world, although there is a *Wulfen* and a *Wulfrath* in Germany and Mason "spoke with an accent."

The first post office was established at Wulfert, February 2, 1897, with Jennie Doane as first postmaster.[2] There just may have been an error made in the name at that time—if Jennie had misspelled it or shortened it for convenience.

Like the areas of the Light House and of Tarpon Bay, Wulfert was isolated by land, dependent upon the waters for transportation and communication. For a long time mail and express had to be taken out to the bulkhead offshore where the steamer could leave and pick up cargo and mail. Settlers had to row out and fetch them ashore.

In the 1890's Dwight put an ad in a Texas newspaper for a partner to help him clear land and set out an orange grove at Wulfert. One named Holloway read it and hied for Sanibel. He had been born in Toronto, Canada, in 1845 and gone to Texas when he was twenty years old. Now he traveled to Tampa, Florida, and eventually in a hired sailboat arrived at Wulfert.

Dwight was married. His Wulfert home had been built by an itinerant ship's carpenter and was so strong it withstood time and hurricanes. (It still stands near the Captiva bridge, where it was moved in later years.) The Dwights and Holloway were so isolated that at first they thought they were the only inhabitants of the island, but they started clearing the land.

For a long time, Holloway remained a bachelor, then he put an ad for a wife in the upriver paper. The reply received came from "a lady out west" who admitted she had tuberculosis and wanted to migrate to Florida "for her health."

Disgusted, the bachelor in his broad Canadian accent told Mason Dwight: "I don't want to marry a dommed inval-id!" He stressed the last syllable vehemently. In late life, he married a lady who was employed in Miss Flossie Hill's "Department Store" in the upriver village.

Dwight and Holloway remained partners for many years. The former farmed. The latter managed their big all-purpose store on the dock, which handled express and mail as the years passed.

Across the rude counter, farmer customers bought necessities of the day. There was a convenient hole cut in the floor

83

In early days, a "bulkhead" meant a sturdy building set upon sturdier pilings offshore at the edge of a deep water channel. To them, the big steamers came via the channels and unloaded cargo, mail and passengers. Farmers and homesteaders would row or sail out to the bulkheads and pick up whatever they had ordered. There was a bulkhead offshore from Wulfert and another offshore from Captiva, as above.—Photo from Scotia Bryant

so they could drop a half-eaten tomato or an orange peel into the water below where it was whisked away by the tide—all the while idly chattering with neighbors they seldom saw except on steamer days.

The first postmaster, Jennie Doane, it was said, never ceased to be a Northerner. She lived in a little fairy-tale house for nearly fifty years and only left Wulfert once. That time, she boarded one of the little steamers and sailed up to the village of Fort Myers to purchase herself some records for her new cylinder Edison phonograph—she wanted to hear the records before she bought them.

In the 1920's, after most of the old-timers were gone from Wulfert, Jennie Doane had a beautiful flower garden and the newcomers to Sanibel would go there to buy flowers and "borrow" cuttings from her with which to start their own island gardens.

About 1904, Frank L. Henderson came in from Port Tampa City on a chartered sailboat. He bought the Bancroft homestead of seventy-five acres at Wulfert and farmed. The only neighbors his daughter, Mrs. Annie Henderson Allred, could recall in recent time were: the Dinkins, the Holloways, the Dwights, and Jennie Doane.[3] As a little girl, Annie had gone to the Wulfert school across Dinkins Bayou. In her old age, a widow, she returned and built a neat modern home among roses by the bayou and is content.

While some of the early settlers returned, others never went away. For six generations the Halls, Hunters, and Gibsons—their children and grandchildren—have lived on Sanibel. Their roots go far back into early America.

Amanta Gibson started out from Sumter County, Florida, then moved to Safety Harbor on Tampa Bay in the wilderness. His father had been out to Missouri and Arkansas, and been a Pony Express rider during that service's brief, exciting day.

Amanta left the Tampa Bay wilds to come by boat to Sanibel and "get him a homestead," for by that time he and his wife, Clementine, had children named Mamie, Bessie, Linnie, and Arthur. They arrived at Wulfert on January 6, 1900.

Here, in the balmy air of island winter, they set up their stove out of doors and Clementine cooked their first meal: It was "tomato gravy" and "hoecake," but it tasted as fine as a royal banquet anywhere.[4]

Clementine diced white bacon and fried it brown and the delicious odor, mingled with the sunlit, salt-tanged air around the Bay tantalized the waiting hungry new arrivals. They watched impatiently while she cut Sanibel tomatoes fine and added them to the bits of sizzling bacon, cooking them together thoroughly. Then, she added water and thickened the well-seasoned gravy. Other times she would add milk but she had none yet.

Southerners usually make "hoecake" with cornmeal. The Gibsons used flour. Amanta's granddaughter will tell you how:

"You put flour in a deep pan, add salt, sugar, a little shortening (less than for regular bread), add milk, if you have

The Gibson family's packinghouse near Wulfert long ago. All the family worked. Neighbors shared labor: one day, a group of neighboring farmers would come help the Gibsons pick vegetables, another day they would help the neighbors. Packing was accomplished in the same manner—each one "pitching in" to help the other. Working together leisurely made work pleasant.

Pictured above is Bessie Gibson (she built excellent tomato crates), next is Mamie Gibson, then, Clementine Gibson, Linnie Gibson, Amanta Gibson, and young Henry Hall who was being "brought up" by the Gibsons. In the driver's seat and standing

it, if not, water. When the dough is ready to bake, it will have a 'certain feel.' Then, you spread it into a heated iron skillet and place a tight lid over it and another under it, 'to form air space and prevent burning.' "

Such "hoecake" deliciously browned and served with the above "tomato gravy" was savory any time of the day. For the hungry brood of Gibsons that first day at Wulfert, it was sheer delight, one they never forgot.

Like most island homesteaders, the Gibsons promptly began erection of a palm-thatched shelter and a palm-thatched kitchen. The floors were of sand covered with clean white seashells from the Gulf shore. In those days, they could sink a barrel in the sands and dip up drinking water almost anywhere on the islands. Such water was a little hard but tasted better than rainwater, and later Matthews Hall got a fine deep well of sweet water.

Arthur Gibson, age twelve, soon learned to fish with a cast net. Other food sources were Sanibel rabbits found everywhere and gophers. Shellfish and turtles, oysters and clams abounded. A family garden was planted.

Amanta went to work for Dwight and Holloway on their farm but later the family "struck out on their own."

There were difficulties, of course. Once the hot sun "burned up" their cabbages. During a very dry spell of weather another time they found their cabbage patch in ruins because raccoons had gone into every head seeking water. When the wind came from offshore, mosquitoes were a plague.

At such times, the Gibsons and others living in palm-thatched homes used heavy smudges of buttonwood to drive the pests away. A few settlers had cheesecloth coverings at their window openings and kept a heavy smudge by their door openings to keep them out. Other homesteaders hung mosquito bars or canopies over each bed so they could sleep in peace.

Swinging close up under the palmetto-thatched roof inside, a few had a cheesecloth "canopy" to keep scorpions and other pests from dropping down unexpectedly.

Around Wulfert, when mosquitoes were particularly bad, farmers cut down cabbage palms and set the roots afire so that horses and mules could huddle around in the smoke and keep mosquitoes at bay. When the wind blew inland—as it did most of the time—all was well and islanders then thought up tall tales about their insects.

Once a stranger came to the islands, Flora Morris will tell you with twinkling eyes. He had with him a big iron cook pot and a carpenter's hammer. Mosquitoes were so bad at that time that the stranger overturned his pot and crawled under it for protection.

The Sanibel mosquitoes stung him right through the iron pot. So the stranger grabbed up his hammer and clenched their stingers over, on the inside of the pot where he was hiding.

But the man lost his pot. The Sanibel mosquitoes flew away with it.

The Wulfert area, strictly a farming community, was not so "genteel" as the Gulf front but it had its interesting characters.

There was Hell Roarin' Smith. No one ever found out much about him. He just moved in, told nothing, built a cheekee, bought a mule, and went to farming.

Usually he started work before sunup. He would yell at his little old mule and cuss and swear as if he were mad at the lonely universe.

The little mule would keep plodding along, while Smith's quarreling voice could be heard all around the scattered community in the stillness of the island air.

So, in time the disturbed but good humored neighbors dubbed him "Hell Roarin' Smith" and let him alone.

And there were the Jennys—good people, Germans—but the man and woman both had bad tempers.

Once, she threw the old man's clothing out into the yard. Another time, when she ordered an iron cookstove and he began to put it together he somehow broke a piece.

Angrily, he picked up an axe and broke up the whole stove, shouting at it in fury: "You start . . . I finish!"

Captain J. J. Dinkins, a diminutive man of the sea, came to raise groves. In time while homesteaders worked their fields and gardens, the spring air was perfumed over Indian mound and ancient mangrove jungle around Wulfert on the bay with the fragrance of orange, grapefruit, and lime blossoms.

Chapter 12[1]

Captiva area's ups and downs . . .

Buck Key, about a mile and a half long, across the narrow channel from Captiva Island, was first settled by William H. Binder. A somewhat puny fellow, he had been a sergeant in the Austrian army and spoke German. At one time he was shipwrecked in nearby waters and found his way to Buck Key and Captiva. There he regained his health, and as a consequence, never left the area again.

The H. G. Brainards were among the first settlers on Buck Key. They came to farm in 1896 and became lifelong friends with Binder.

Who was Captiva's first homesteader? That is a question. H. G. Brainard's son claimed to be the first settler, some say. Binder claimed to be the first homesteader. He did build a home there later, and he had the previous statement chiseled onto his tombstone.

Regardless of which was first, the subsequent best known farmers were the Carters, the Kennons, and the Bryants.

George W. Carter, a Floridian, and his wife, Elizabeth, from Georgia, homesteaded on Captiva about 1900. George's father had been an Indian fighter. When the Carters arrived there was no road and there were no homesteaders—only some Spanish Indian fishermen on their part of the island. For some time, they went to Cayo Costa (which had a post office called "Boca Grande"), or to Punta Gorda via sailboat to obtain mail and supplies.

The Carters raised eggplants, tomatoes, and peppers for market which they shipped out by boat. They also had a home garden for table use and to sell to rich winter tourists who came by in fancy yachts in winter.

Later, the Carters set out a grapefruit and orange grove, avocado trees, and more coconut palms.

All this, with a little hunting and fishing, made them a good living. In a short time, they had a long dock built out over the waters so they could ship surplus produce and fruits direct.

The Walter F. Mickle family settled about a mile beyond the Carters, but meanwhile the Robert A. Kennons moved to Captiva from the deep wilds of the Big Cypress Indian country. They lived in a palm-thatched cheekee while they homesteaded land.

Also the Granville Worthington Bryants moved down from Inverness, Florida. When the big steamer was moored to the dock, Hunter Bryant saw nothing of the settlers on the wharf

Typical sailboat of yesterday with Mrs. E. S. Everett and G. W. Lewis aboard, near residence of G. M. Ormsby, off Buck Key, Florida. It was possible to live on one part of an island for some time and not know others lived elsewhere on the same one. But islanders soon learned to sail and row and explore and get acquainted.—Photo courtesy Scotia Bryant

90

Thatched homestead on Captiva in a hammock of sabal palms. Gordon Brainard is on the extreme right, the others are unknown. Early homesteaders sometimes made hearth fires on little mounds of earth and cooked in Dutch ovens and iron kettles. Later they had modest pioneer houses of wood with tiny kitchens.—Old Press photo about 1903

or the seagulls winging above the choppy blue waters—he saw only the Kennon girls.

To his brother, Karl, he said: "There's the girl for me!" At the same moment Karl looking at Rosa Kennon said: "She's for me!"

They were young and they were joking but it wasn't long before they were married by a Methodist minister who sailed from Fort Myers down the river and up Bay and Sound to their homestead and married them to the girls they had picked on the day of their arrival.

The Bryants and the Kennons farmed. At first they

The old Carter homestead on Captiva. Someone, name unknown, had lived on the land before the Carters and failed to "prove up" their claim. Outside the homes, stiff brooms of sedge were used to make a clearing. Brooms used inside were not so stiff. The buildings above later became part of Chadwick's coconut grove, which still later became the South Seas Plantation.—Old Press photo about 1903

shipped out by schooner because the steamer could not land nearby. Later they shipped via the Captiva bulkhead, and at last via the Kinzie Line.

The Captiva Post Office was established August 29, 1901. Granville Hunter Bryant was first postmaster. It was on the Captiva bulkhead to which residents rowed or sailed for it was about a half a mile from shore.

Settlers arrived on the island by devious ways. When Robert Knowles was six months old, his father fetched him from Inverness, Florida (from whence the Bryants had come), to Punta Gorda where the railroad ended. The baby had been laid on a pillow in their covered wagon so he could watch the flapping of the canvas cover and be content.

In Punta Gorda the parents sold the covered wagon to pay steamboat fare to Captiva. When they arrived on the island they had only fifty cents left, and that was used to buy a hoe, for the father went to work for Tobe Bryant at once.

The Knowles family lived at the Tobe Bryant's until they could build a cheekee. The newly thatched home smelled clean and had a floor of white beach sand covered with seashells to keep down dust.

After a while Knowles began to cut buttonwood, load it into a sailboat and deliver it upriver for sale in the village of Myers. Sometimes the mother and child went along. They would put a mattress on the deck and all sleep there at night under the stars. They cooked on board by building a fire in a box of sand. It sometimes took a whole week to go and come for they sailed by the wind and the tide.

Shortly after the turn of the century, Knowles moved over to Buck Key where his father had homesteaded and built a house on the side of a dock out over the water. Young Robert Knowles played on the dock with a little girl named Ann Brainard whose family was already living there.

When the Captiva Post Office was moved ashore, March 20, 1903, Hattie E. Brainard, formerly of Buck Key, became postmaster while her husband continued to farm.

Several of the Brainard babies died before and after birth; and Brainard met a tragic death. On his farm several Negroes had been working. One day there was an argument during

93

Working on the Carter homestead *circa* 1897-1898. Left to right: George W. Carter, Jesse and Knight Carter, Alpine Carter, Mrs. George Carter and James Carter. Note papayas and coconuts already bearing.

When homesteaders went anywhere, they walked or rowed or sailed. Kerosene lamps and candles furnished light but most of them went to bed at sundown.—Old Press photo

Captiva vegetables at "pickin" time, ready to be taken to the packinghouse, then to the wharf to be shipped by the paddle-wheel steamers to the outside world. Workers unidentified.

In their home gardens, these farmers raised cabbages, string beans, peas, potatoes, lettuce, a few watermelons, cantaloupes, squash, pumpkins, turnips, even cauliflower and kohlrabi and later sold some of their surplus to the Gulf front inns when they gradually came into being.—Old Press photo about 1903

which one of the hired men struck Brainard with a grub hoe. In three days he was dead; and for years afterward, no Negroes were allowed on the island.

Hattie continued to operate the post office. It was said that she "set an excellent table," serving bacon, fried chicken, fish, loaf bread, biscuit bread, rice, and garden vegetables. She made her own yeast out of cornmeal and cut it into squares which were dried and hung up in bags. Sometimes she used "potato water and made delicious potato bread."

Some time later, she married a man named Gore. Under the name of Hattie E. Gore, she continued to operate the Captiva Post Office from December 21, 1916, until 1940—*37 years altogether!*

Long before, another settler in Captiva was Belton Johnson, who moved up from Sanibel with his father. Belton remembers how they could dig a hole back from the shore and obtain drinking water. "It would be in a sand strand" rather than among seashells, for there rainwater would come

95

In the above photograph, taken about 1900, is (standing) James Carter, two unknowns, George W. Carter, Knight Carter, Tobe Bryant and Jesse Carter. Sitting down are Lawrence, Knight and Jim Sirman. The boy is Buddy Curry; the girl, Ollie Curry. The women are Mrs. G. W. Carter, Alpine and Mamie Carter. Babies in high chairs are unidentified.

Contrary to legend, the Chadwicks did not plant the first palms on Captiva. When the Carter family homesteaded there, some coconuts were already thriving, original owners unknown. The Carters planted more about 1900, and again in 1910. By 1919, the palms were too tall to climb.—Photo courtesy Scotia Bryant

seeping through from the island's interior toward the Gulf and the purified water was sweet and fine to drink.

Belton and his father gathered quantities of young white ibis for food. These they killed and while fresh salted them down to draw the blood. Then they were washed and re-salted to preserve them, and they kept fine without ice.

Salted ibis were de-salted for use later by soaking them in fresh water. Thereafter they could be made into fine stew, or floured and fried to be served with gravy and steamed rice, or used cold fried for a quick lunch aboard their boat.

Loggerhead turtles ate horseshoe crabs and crustaceans and had a lot of meat but it was in small amounts in various parts

96

of their bodies. Loggerheads were captured in a turtle net. Their bits of meat were ground up like hamburger, onion and seasonings added, and fried in thin cakes until done.

The Johnsons preferred green turtle for turtle steaks. These turtles were vegetarians and had a better flavor than the loggerheads, also more meat.

They used a barrel for a "smokehouse" and smoked fish and roe. They salted mullet and hung it up in the rigging of their boat to sun and air dry there. They also sun dried turtle meat, which they called "jerked turtle" (probably after the "jerky beef" used by men of the Punta Rassa cattle trail across Carlos Bay).

Mosquitoes? Captiva fishermen burned old nets and stood in the smoke when they were very bad. Fishing guides used Bee Brand Powder as a smudge aboard their yachts, and buttonwood smoke ashore.

Islanders who were eventually fortunate enough to have glass windows would go around their house from room to room at twilight with a smoke pot or smudge—each adult or child checking a window or poking under a bed to drive the pests finally out the open door.

Was there a boatbuilder on the islands? There was not. A settler drove in a nail or added a patch when and where it was needed. He sewed his own sails and patched them when they needed it.

Was there a barber on the islands? There was none.

What did they do for haircuts and shaves? They cut each other's hair, shaved themselves.

What did they charge for the haircuts?

Blank amazement: "Nothing. Nothing at all. That's the way it was then."

How about a blacksmith? Didn't they need one to put shoes on the mules and horses for the farmers of the islands? "Nope. Didn't need shoes. Creatures walked on soft sandy trails or along the sandy shore."

That's the way that it *was*. . . .

Small tales of Captiva have come down through the years, like the day Circuit Rider George Gatewood went fishing

The tiny post office on Captiva. Hattie Brainard Gore was postmaster there for thirty-seven years. Her early home was very small, having only two rooms, and children had to climb over a heavy sill to clamber inside. The floor was of sand. But she had fetched hand-painted china, some silver, and hand-carved picture frames in which were portraits of her English and Canadian kindred. They made strange contrast with the rude homemade pioneer furniture and sandy floor of early life on Captiva Island.—Photo courtesy Irving R. Latham

with Gordon Brainard before the latter "died." (No one ever said he was killed.)

Gatewood and Brainard sailed along and came across William Binder, the Austrian homesteader who was in the water, outside his boat, clinging to it and obviously in some kind of trouble.

Directly, they saw that inside Binder's boat was a six-foot tarpon, floundering about in wild leaps of silver fury. Amazed, they asked Binder what had happened.

He said the huge fish had jumped into his boat, so he had jumped out.

As Binder clung to his boat and talked in his broken English, the rescuers who had come upon him laughed long and loud. When a fish takes a boat from a man, that was a pretty good story!

Cheerfully they helped Binder into their boat and towed his boat and fish along to Captiva. There, they all generously shared tarpon steaks for supper among the homesteaders in their immediate area.

There were other early settlers scattered over Captiva in the early days—Dr. W. S. Turner, John A. Frow, the Dickeys—but the Bernard Eybers were "city people" and thought they were alone in their island world on the bay.

The Eybers (Frederick and Clara, with Lottie, nineteen, and Richard, sixteen) had come from Germany to New York. There Frederick became ill. Hearing of the healthful Florida islands, he sent Richard to look around and received a letter back saying that "anything more would be Paradise."

So, the Eybers decided to move south. Unlike most homesteaders, they fetched a freight car of furniture along to Punta Gorda. There, the furniture was loaded aboard the side-wheeler *St. Lucie,* and sailed down Charlotte Harbor and Pine Island Sound to the Captiva bulkhead.

From that offshore building on pilings, their possessions were removed to a smaller boat that headed for the shore. Anchored offshore, poles were laid from the boat to the land, and the crated and uncrated belongings were carefully rolled and slid on round logs laid across long poles to the shore.

Gradually the Eybers' belongings were moved up to the

Early homesteaders of Captiva and relatives at a family get-together. Left to right: Karl Ashton Bryant, Scotia Bryant, Granville Bryant. On steps, R. A. Kennon. In rocker on porch, Mrs. Karl (Rosa Kennon) Bryant, holding Kenneth Bryant, Mrs. May Brainard, holding Beulah Brainard (later Mrs. Beulah Wiles), Mable Kennon, Mrs. Ed. (Belle) Kennon, holding Margaret Kennon. Standing by the post is Warner Bryant, then Mrs. Hunter Bryant, holding Ruby Bryant.

The boy on the top step is G. H. Bryant. Next to post, right, is Edward Kennon, holding P. J. Kennon, and seated on the porch is Hunter Bryant.—Photo courtesy Scotia Bryant

two-story house they had bought. It was built high to escape storm tides and it was no easy task. Moreover, there were dense mangrove jungles that prevented their seeing far in any direction.

Many things frightened these city settlers who were aliens in a strange tropical land but the loneliness was the hardest to bear. And their first Christmas, despite birds singing and flowers blooming by the waters, was the loneliest that they would ever know.

They did not know there were farmers elsewhere on the island. There were no bright lights, no decorated Christmas trees. So, in the night, they rowed out over the dark waters of the pass and to break the unbearable emptiness of the warm fragrant night, they (all but Frederick) began to sing Christmas carols.

They sang in their native German for it comforted them, and the singing helped ease their being so lost and alone. At last they began to sing: "Silent Night, Holy Night."

And as their song reached out across the dark waters, from the darker jungles of the island across the way, they thought they heard the sound of an instrument echoing their song.

What strange communication! It could not be! Yet, as they sang on, verse after verse, and paused to listen—there was the sound of a flute echoing them.

Excitedly they rowed toward the sounds as if drawn by an unseen magnet in the night. And when they finished their song, they started over again for fear of losing contact.

When their boat reached the far shore, out from the shadows of Buck Key came the Austrian, William Binder, with a flute. "I heard you sing," he cried. "You sing my language . . . but I could not make you hear me call in the wind . . . so I ran and got my flute . . . so you would know I was here."

The lonely settlers cried with joy that they had found each other in the far away island world on Christmas.

And that, too, was the way it was around Captiva and Buck Key long ago.

Chapter 13

L.H. problems, war, and St. Patrick's Day . . .

The first island farmers planted in early spring and harvested in April and May. Once they learned the climatic advantages of Sanibel (that there was no winter, no need to wait for spring), they planted and harvested from early fall until the next June, or as long as market prices held up.

On July 3, 1888, all island land had been released, except Sections 20, 21, and 29, so that the homesteaders could perfect their titles.[1] But more settlers wanted to buy or homestead and there was only one large tract left: the 668 acres of the Light House Reservation, which extended from the point to what is now Bailey's Road.

In 1885 the upriver *Press* had described Point Ybel as being high, with miles of shell roads, "some walks, some broad carriage ways. . . . In many places . . . bordered with flowers and grass as if planted so." There was no grass on the shell roads, they were "graded like a turnpike as left by action of water during a hurricane at least a thousand years ago. . . ."

That description applied only to the immediate vicinity of Point Ybel, however, not to Sections 20, 21, and 29. These adjoined each other and contained prairie-type land, carpeted green, dotted with sabal palms and wild flowers. Little clearing would be necessary to utilize it, so it was coveted by many.

Even before the Light House had been established, the Honorable Mr. Cameron had written the L.H. Board that the Honorable M. S. Quay of Pennsylvania wished "to purchase all of Sanibel . . . not needed for L.H. purposes."[2] Islander

Bullock, May 28, 1889, asked the board "when will this Reservation be thrown open to the public?" and islander Ed Pell, May 29, 1889, asked permission to occupy and farm part of the land.

The L.H. Board directed its engineer to tell them "no," and to urge Light House keeper, Shanahan, to keep trespassers off the three sections.

Still, during 1892, 1893, and 1894, a Mr. Saxon wanted to locate there; a Mr. Bryant wished to plant five hundred acres of castor beans; a Mr. McCall wanted it open to homesteading; and an American Invalid Aid Society requested five hundred acres for "benevolent purposes."

In 1896 it was "discovered" that the Matthews Wharf and warehouse had encroached on the L.H. Reservation. The board decided to make the wharf legal by deeding it to the public, then it officially surveyed its remaining land and fenced it off with barbed wire.[3]

That did not stop new settlers from coming. About 1896, Frank Padgett arrived upriver by steamer and set out from the village of Fort Myers with stock and equipment bound for Sanibel to farm. He drove down the sandy, lonesome trail to Punta Rassa, camping at what is now Iona along the way.

At Punta Rassa, Frank loaded his stock and equipment aboard Captain Granville's schooner. They sailed across Carlos Bay and landed at Reed's. He was invited to dine with the family and met Reed's son, Will, and daughter, Lucy—and millions of mosquitoes, gnats, and sand flies. The drinking water smelled and tasted of sulphur.

Padgett asked if anyone else was living in so desolate a place. Reed said, "Yes," took a chaw of Sensation Tobacco, and told him about homesteaders and settlers living in scattered locales around the islands.

Astonished, Frank inquired if they were "dodging the law, or escaped convicts, or what?" Reed said the climate, fishing and healthful surroundings had brought them—the fine crops and good incomes caused them to remain.

So Padgett remained. He rented an old barn and moved in. One shed had a loft used for sleeping that was reached by climbing up a rude ladder nailed to the wall. He arranged for

Top: The early home of Frank and E. R. Bailey, farmers, when they came to Carlos Bay on Sanibel to raise luscious Sanibel Island tomatoes that became famous in the North in winters of the 1890's.

Below: A little later, the home of the Baileys, after they had established the Sanibel Packing Company and added mercantile business to farming.—Courtesy Eleanor Pearse estate

George E. Schultz, manager, in telegraph office at Punta Rassa across from Sanibel, where the first news of the sinking of the Battleship *Maine* was received on the mainland of the United States, February 15, 1898.— Old Press photo about 1903

fertilizer and supplies to come by steamer and tried to start planting his first twenty-five acres.

Work was impossible at first because of insects. Smudges and mosquito brushes were used against them by day; a mosquito net covered the bed or was suspended above the pallet at night.

Then, the wind changed. The insects were blown away. As it became cooler, the plants grew fine. Frank hired a male cook. They did their own washing. During the day, they picked tomatoes, at night they packed them for shipment by steamer the next day. Frank wrote friends and relatives he had found "The Eldorado."

When the Reverend Mr. Barnes was on a trip to Kentucky to extoll the marvels of Sanibel, two brothers, Frank P. and Ernest Bailey, of Virginia heard him and came south to farm. They located not far from Matthews Wharf. In later times, they somehow leased the entire Light House Reservation, except for small portions otherwise leased at the time. Rentals varied from $400 to $515 per annum, and the lease stipulated that the Baileys could erect buildings, etc., to facilitate

105

cultivation of the land but at the expiration of the agreement all such improvements were to revert to the United States.[4]

In 1899 when young ladies of the island packed the vegetables for shipments that went out over the Matthews Wharf by daily steamers, the Bailey brothers saw the need for a packing and mercantile center. They established the Sanibel Packing Company and general store at the head of the Matthews dock.

So the smells of leather, vinegar, and spices came to vie with vanilla and coffee on old Carlos Bay. There was, at Bailey's, green coffee to be roasted and ground or packaged new varieties. A big wooden meat block stood on ponderous legs, with meat cleavers hanging within ready reach on the wall. Harness and all sorts of needs for farmers' wagons, horses, mules, and men were on hand. Sugar and many supplies came in barrels. Lamps and lanterns hung from the ceiling. Kerosene was in bulk tanks outside.

(When ice came in around 1910, it was sold in big blocks packed in sawdust to prevent melting, and ice cream was made and sold.)

Bailey's supplies, large and small, arrived by the steamers and were delivered over the dock. Customers came to ship produce over the wharf and bought supplies at the store instead of writing to Punta Gorda for later shipment.

But islanders did not go often, for their little farms, usually three to five acres in extent, were scattered along what is now Periwinkle Drive, Tarpon Bay Road and on up the island toward Blind Pass and Captiva, and the trip was not always easy.

The George M. Coopers were farming, and had a boat business on Tarpon Bay. Their home was on the Tarpon Bay Road. Their granddaughter, Genevieve, was born at the Sanibel Light House when her mother was visiting there, and when she grew old enough, she attended Miss Lettie Nutt's island school.

James Hugh Johnson, the father of Belton Johnson, had come from Lake Placid, Florida, where he had had a homestead. He came down the Sound from Punta Gorda on the big stern-wheeler, and got started by picking tomatoes for the

106

Captain Hand, commander of the U.S. Revenue Cutter *McLain*, during the Spanish-American War off Sanibel and Charlotte Harbor waters.— Courtesy Eleanor Pearse Estate

Bailey brothers. He liked the island so well he sold his upstate homestead and returned to sharecrop with Captain James Ashmore, the brother of Mrs. Laetitia Nutt.

There were heavy cultivations going on at Wulfert, and grove plantings on Buck Key, and farming had spread to Captiva.

In the meantime, around these islands and the lower Florida Keys, after about 1895, filibusters had been operating against Cuba. Spain had sent troops to "put down the insurrection" among the citizens there; and the United States at length sent its Battleship *Maine* to Havana Harbor.

To Punta Rassa across ancient Carlos Bay from Sanibel on February 15, 1898, came the sudden and amazing news that the big battleship had been sunk in Havana Harbor!

Over the telegraph wires up the Caloosa Hatchee, north to Jacksonville, and on to Washington went the news. In a short time, 25,000 troops were assembling at Tampa. The North American Squadron made rendezvous at old Tortugas Harbor and Key West. The Revenue Cutter *McLain,* with Captain Hand, arrived off Sanibel to guard the Bay and Harbor.

Sanibel Island, its southern coast in almost direct line with

107

Havana and its surrounding waters known to the Spaniards for centuries got special attention.

The U.S. Signal Corps took over.[5] Cable huts of corrugated iron, about eight feet square, were set up—one at Point Ybel, the other about midway of the island on the Gulf front. The hut on the south shore had a cable coming in from the Gulf. A conduit, with one cable, connected the two huts on the island. The one midway of the island had a cable running to Punta Rassa. A signal tower stood at this midway point on the island and soldiers were kept on watch and patrolled the telegraph lines.

Over at Punta Rassa, quadruple wires were hastily strung overland and up the river and they were continuously patrolled, for the telegraph was then the only communications link there was.

At the same time, the Spanish fisheries were once more suspected of being collaborators with the enemy. At night, small boats would be seen sailing out from the mouths of the rivers, crossing Charlotte Harbor or Carlos Bay. On sighting another ship, they would hastily douse their lights and vanish into the darkness.[6]

The U.S. Revenue Cutter *McLain*, patrolling waters of Carlos Bay and Charlotte Harbor during the Spanish-American War in 1898.—Photo National Archives

This was the modest little Spanish-American War, that lasted only a hundred and fourteen days.

When it was over, the soldiers, the Signal Corps and the Revenue Cutter all went away. The islanders resumed what had never been left off—their own easygoing way of life that was beginning to emerge as a pattern for future generations.

As an example of their tolerance (or was it a fine excuse to have a party?) they cheerfully celebrated St. Patrick's Day although practically all of them were Protestants.[7]

"At ten o'clock, Mr. Woodring's boat left the wharf with a merry party that was chaperoned by Mrs. Will Matthews, organizer of the excursion," wrote a visiting Catholic participant. "A little later, a half a dozen crowded vehicles bore across the prairie with those who preferred the overland route.

"Riders and sailors, most of them adorned with green badges, met at Dwight's Landing (Wulfert), one of the loveliest spots on the island. The day was perfect. The sky cloudless, the sea like glass and rowing was fine. Northern guests preferred to wander through the woods and were especially attracted by the beautiful coconut trees, some in full bearing.

"All enjoyed a delicious luncheon: oysters, hot and cold, raw, roasted, and fried. All men opened oysters, all rowed boats. The women let them do the work.

"After dark, a campfire was kindled and the effect was artistic as excursionists stood around it, singing plantation songs.

" 'Way Down Upon the Suwannee River' was especially effective for a low wind had sprung up and the sound of the outgoing tide seemed an accompaniment set in a low minor key.

"Not until the moon had risen above the treetops did the party start home. At first there was jest and laughter, but gradually the crowd became rather silent: perhaps touched by the beauty of the semi-tropical land and sky that a full moon and light, drifting clouds idealized . . .

"Perhaps for the first time that day they realized the significance with half-amused, half-sad sense of how the passing present obscures the past, and how little, despite green

109

ribbons, they had really thought of Ireland, her crimes and follies, wrongs and sufferings, genius and heroism on that, her National Day—or of Father Ryan's beautiful verses:

Crown unto the jewels of tears
    The brow of the Celt's great day
And out of the woes of the years—
    Out of the wrongs of a thousand years—
That have swept all her freedom away—
    Weave a mantle as dark as the cloud."

The "Wearin' o' the Green," the appreciation of the Confederate Stars and Bars, and the glory of the U.S. Stars and Stripes were mingled together and accepted as part of the happy life of the islands.

Chapter 14

Book learnin' by the sea . . .

What mattered it that the tides kept their endless rhythmic schedule and there was immensity of starlit heavens at night? The homesteaders' children needed "learnin'" and that was that.

However, Lee County had only been cut off from Monroe in 1887. The islands had been opened for homesteading in 1888. Clusters of children were living at Point Ybel, around Tarpon Bay, on the open Gulf, and a few were scattered along the mid-island. There was clamoring for a school in 1889.

When the islanders petitioned the school board[1] for a school, it was suggested that they give a site for the building, bond title for same, and the board would furnish material for a school—provided the settlers would construct it at their own expense.

That was September 4, 1889. A month later, the board specified that the school should be "sixteen by twenty-four by twelve feet, of rough lumber—up and down board siding, all heart wood—battened outside. Flooring blocks and sills are to be of hard wood. There should be a door and four windows."[2]

The board said the school "should be placed where originally planned," complaining that Mrs. Nutt had disagreed with them as to the location and failed "to comply with her promise of building a school on the beach."

The homesteaders wanted their school about a mile and a half from the Light House "near the landing on San Carlos Bay," instead of on "George Fitzhugh's land," because it would soon be necessary to establish another school several miles from the landing.

In December, a petition was made by the Nutts for a school to be conducted "in a room in a private home on Sanibel." This may have been in the Nutt home, or in the Fitzhugh home, as children were taught in both at different times.

The school board finally ordered lumber for a school on May 31, 1890, and sent a representative over to select a site. It was a mile and a half back from the landing near Richard Adler's. Adler gave the land June 12, 1890, according to deed records of Lee County and this school seems to have been built. Yet a year later, on petition of the islanders on June 27, it was "to be moved, provided the island settlers paid for it and that desks and other school property was moved—at their own expense."[3]

By December 26, 1891, Miss Lettie Nutt was teaching in the "West Sanibel School," for $2.50 per pupil per term. Records of November 3, 1892, disclose that three students were taking Latin, one geometry, three algebra, and two were anxious to go to college. That year, although it had no flags, the Sanibel school had celebrated Columbus Day in October.

Early records show that school was often taught in a special room in a home and the teacher paid by the board until a building could be erected. Old-timers say that sometimes a teacher could be hired for as few as five students; at other times the number was fifteen. In later years, John Boring, at Blind Pass, had a small school in his packing shed where his own and a few other children were taught by a private teacher.

Mrs. Belle Boyd, mother-in-law of Bill Towles of the up-river village, was said to have had "good success" with the Sanibel school in 1893 but in September 1894, the schoolhouse was blown down in a hurricane. E. T. Pell was "awarded $43 to erect a new school [a year later], to be located on his property." He was paid $54.50 for the job when it was completed.

Only four months thereafter, February 4, 1895, the board voted to "discontinue the Sanibel school." No reason given.

The first Sanibel School House was built on the Bailey Road at the edge of the Light House Reservation. This one was next and stood east of where Clarence Rutland lives now. Later this was moved some distance west of Rutland's and "additions and improvements" made.

This photograph was made by Leona Hamilton Howell, when she came to Sanibel to teach, September 1924. She was welcomed by islanders and the Webb Shanahan's at Palm Lodge with a "delightful evening of dancing and dainty refreshments." In November, the Sanibel School had a grand picnic with most of the islanders joining in.

The belfry above shown disappeared in a hurricane. The building is now the Pirate's Theatre.—Photo courtesy Leona Hamilton Howell

Eight months afterward, July 26, 1896, a bid was accepted for an acre of land at Holt's Place, and a bid of F. H. Parks to build a school there for $460 was accepted. The Pell land above was sold.

At length, the island of Sanibel was divided into two districts by the board. After August 3, 1896, all of Sanibel east of a north-south line running through Section 24 and 25 in Township 46, Range 22, became District 14. West of these sections and this line became Section 16, known as *West Sanibel.* A new school was to be erected in West Sanibel provided deed and property petition were presented by August 6—three days later!

Within twenty-three days, a deed was accepted and recorded by the board from H. D. Rose and B. Shelby. The old school was sold to W. P. Beard and September 26, 1897, F. H. Parks was paid $539 to erect another.

Mrs. Laetitia A. Nutt was teaching "in the Matthews Section," West Sanibel in April 1901. The East Sanibel school had been closed and another promised for fall. Then this East Sanibel school was moved to a "more favorable location." And around 1902, H. G. Head moved it to a square acre that was purchased from George N. Riddle and his wife.

School records fail to clearly indicate the location of these schools. The Loveland manuscript does not clearly explain how many were "built." Living old-timers disagree about the authenticity of all the records. It is apparent that the settlers of one section of the island were not always aware of what was going on. Perhaps they were too young to remember.

All Sanibel islanders agree that the first school they remember was located on the old Bailey Road, just outside the Light House Reservation. Among living children, now grown old, who attended this school are: Lucy Jenny, Anna Meade, Belton Johnson, Charlotta and Clark Matthews (until Charlotta went back North), the Woodrings, and others.

Homesteaders of the Tarpon Bay area laid a plank path through the mangrove swamp around the shore of Carlos Bay and a small footlog across an opening near Woodring's, so their children could walk around the Bay to the school.

One little boy was late for school because his grandmother—a newcomer—made him wait ever so often as they trudged together through the jungles until multitudes of fiddler crabs scrambled with great and fearful (to them) clatter out of their way.

This first remembered public schoolhouse was moved up to the road that rambled through the center of the island (Periwinkle Drive today) by Tom Hand. It soon became too small as many children came from different sections. It was abandoned and became a vegetable packinghouse.[4]

Finally, the school, to which so many homesteaders' children went, was built a little farther on the same road, east of where Clarence Rutland lives today.

Many were the arguments about school buildings and sites. Teachers came and went. But the Nutts and the Matthewses brought always the best education possible under the circumstances to the children of Sanibel. School was often held at The Gables, with Laetitia or one of the girls teaching—even if there were only three or four children. At one time, when there were some Negro children on the island for a while, Miss Cordie Nutt gathered them up and taught them, free, in the Nutt home.

There were a few who complained that the Nutt family never forgot the Confederacy and that was true. Nevertheless, they passed on to the island children a great love for the United States—North and South—following the pattern of General Robert E. Lee who, in defeat, sought only to bind the wounds of war and create statesmen for the good of the future of the nation.

This was often a surprise to strangers. One stranger to Sanibel was amazed to learn that the birthday of the Confederate general was a legal holiday in Florida. Not knowing what to expect, he attended the island school to see what went on that day.[5]

The program, he reported, was largely of the greatness of Lee as man and soldier, one could "almost feel the presence of the grand old man," while other features made the occasion one of "historical and patriotic review."

The schoolhouse was draped in General Lee's colors and otherwise beautifully decorated. The drawings on the blackboard, done by the pupils, were artistic and contained among other things, quotations from Benjamin Franklin, Robert E. Lee, and Stonewall Jackson.

Ceremonies opened with an "Entrance March" by the school and was followed by Psalm XV, and remarks by Miss Lettie Nutt, teacher. Then came the program:

"A biographical sketch, Benjamin Franklin, 5th grade; Memorial Song, school; Memorial Day, Florence Reed; Come Thou With Me, Floretta Riddle; The Sword of Lee, Irene Riddle; remarks, A Private Confederate Soldier; The Silent March, Callena Jenny; Dirge for Ashley, Clarence Cooper; Stonewall Jackson, Luella Chauncey; Come Let Us Cross The River, Marie Jenny; Love Your Country, infant class; The Flag, Harrison Woodring; America, song, audience and

115

school; The Rose From Chancellorville, Lucy Jenny; The Blue and the Gray, Flora Woodring; Jim of Biloxi, Edwin Jenny; Lee to the Rear, Genevieve Cooper; Dixie, audience and school."

The Northern visitor could find no fault with the unusual program. He found the whole "reflecting much credit upon the accomplished teacher and her children. . . ."

The school was the heart of the community. Its pupils, with teacher guidance, were always celebrating something.

Sometimes it closed down at noon, so pupils could prepare special programs that were held there every Friday evening, attended by most of the homesteaders and settlers.

There was a Literary and Debating Society that met there every Saturday. Arbor Day was celebrated each year with the school "appropriately and picturesquely decorated"; settlers and children gathered then to enjoy a dinner "worthy," said the *Press* later, "of the skill and hospitality of Sanibel house-keepers."

New Year's Day was not passed by. In 1900, it was observed with entertainment, games, and shell gathering on the shore. Mrs. Laetitia Nutt and Mrs. Matthews distributed presents and oranges to pupils.

A few days later, Mrs. Matthews received attractive books for the children and Mrs. Nutt added more from "her own book cases." The books were for the East Sanibel school, "provided the settlers arranged a locked case in which to keep them."

Manners were taught judiciously at the gatherings and their mental horizons were expanded by the often splendid visitors who came to the islands. When Rose Cleveland, sister of President Cleveland, came she was invited to attend school and speak with the pupils. So was the Episcopal bishop from Miami. March 7, 1907, the pleasant commencement was given by Miss Lettie Nutt. The children of all ages acted out a varied program and there was a talk given by "a Mr. Kitchen, of Leeds, England, regarding South Africa and Madagascar."

At Wulfert, as early as 1901, homesteaders were asking for a school for "North Sanibel." By May 1, 1902, there were ten families there; Wulfert had become a farming and shipping point. The early request denied, the school board now said if they had fifteen pupils and a home with a room where they could be taught, the county would pay the teacher—if one could be found and a place for him to stay could be located.

A teacher named David Sumner was located. A man named Raulerson or Roberson, living at Bowen's Place agreed to house the school and the teacher until a schoolhouse could be erected.

By July 10 that year, lumber for the Wulfert school was out at the bulkhead offshore.

The homesteaders hauled the lumber ashore, banded together, pitched in, and built the little schoolhouse themselves.

It stood near the Roberson home, on the Wulfert Road, on

To the above Wulfert school about 1904 went Annie Henderson, now Mrs. Annie Allred, daughter of Frank Henderson. The school was located about a mile and a quarter from the present Wulfert-Captiva "turn of the road." The Henderson children crossed Dinkin's Bayou in a rowboat, then walked on to school. The Hendersons had only four neighbors: the J. J. Dinkins, the Holloways, the Dwights, and the Doanes. But other farmers lived farther away and their children, too, walked or rowed and walked to get an education.

This picture, taken in the early 1920's, shows Emmett Brantley and William (Mitch) Mitchell who lived at Ciego or Blind Pass. It hangs on the wall of Mitchell's old home where Stella, his ninety-three-year-old widow, still resides. The Wulfert school burned about 1924.—Photo loaned by Stella Mitchell

117

the left side coming up from the old landing—about a mile from the old warehouse, store and post office—on high ground.[6]

Buck Key, offshore from Captiva, wanted a school as soon as Captain G. M. Ormsby bought a government lot of ninety-one acres. In April 1897, the school board agreed to move the West Sanibel school to Buck Key and employ Ed McIntyre, teacher, at thirty-five dollars a month. This Buck Key school was held in a small outbuilding near Ormsby's home.[7] By late April he claimed it had ten pupils.

The following year, the board authorized opening of this school and employment of a teacher at twenty-five dollars a month, with Miss M. Fannie Porter, teacher. On February 21, she had eight pupils; by April there were twelve. The school closed June 16 and the teacher left, after which there was "quite a party of young people from Buck Key who celebrated by going over to Captiva Beach for an island beef [barbecue]."

The Buck Key school must have continued on in Ormsby's home for the December 27, 1900, *Press* upriver reported:

The first Captiva school, not far from the cemetery on the shell mound by the sea. Repaired and enlarged a little from time to time, the building was the educational center of Captiva. There patriotic observances were held and plays given by the children. Monthly, non-denominational religious services took place, weather permitting, after which there were picnic dinners on the grounds outdoors. The belfry was added many years later.

118

"Buck Key high school (that is, as high as we could get in a two-story house) with four scholars, is taking a vacation and Miss Nutt is going home for the holidays."

A February 1901 note said Miss Nutt entertained her children at Buck Key school with a candy pull and one June 27 said that "school closed with evening session and candy pull. First school of eight months in three years and best teacher in the country!"

At last, there was a school on Captiva. As homesteaders and farmers moved up the island, the schools followed. The one on Captiva opened October 22, 1903, with Lilly White, teacher, but a week later, the school was reported as progressing nicely with teacher, Miss Dewey, "making many friends."

Many years later, there was another school up near Bryant's Place on Captiva.

Meanwhile, in 1910, the school board instructed the Wulfert school to combine with Captiva. The tiny school by the sea was enlarged a little but there was no belfry. There was the tiny cemetery on the shell mound among the quiet trees where Hattie Brainard had buried her beloved daughter, and the songs of birds, and children's voices.

Sometimes there could be no school on Captiva because there was no teacher. Once a picnic was planned at Blind Pass but it couldn't be held because there were not enough boats—and it had to be held beneath the trees that grew around the school.

But somehow, education flourished on the islands.

Some of the island teachers in addition to the Nutt family (Mrs. Laetitia, Miss Cordie, Miss Nannie, and Miss Lettie), and those already mentioned, were:

Miss Katie Adkins, Mrs. W. W. Bailey, W. P. Biggar, Miss Ada Burch, Mrs. Edna K. Burhans, Ruth Carter, L. T. Chambers, J. P. English, Miss Lucille Everedge, Miss Elizabeth Felker, Mrs. Lee Fitzhugh, Miss Elita Fox, Miss Nell Gould, Miss Ethel Goulding, Miss Leona Hamilton, S. H. Hanson, Miss Claude Harrison, Frank Hendry, Miss Nellie Howell, Walter Hughes.

Pauline Johnson, Miss Tabetha Johnson, F. H. Luter, Miss Hazel Magill, Miss Priscilla Peckham, George Rinkle, R. W.

Rivers, J. D. Schell, Mrs. J. L. Shelton, Miss Elaine Smith, Miss Lucy Thomas, Mrs. Mary Waldron, Miss Savannah White, Mrs. T. W. Wiles, Jr., and Stella Belle Wilson.

Chapter 15

Faith, doctorin', and happy days . . .

Surrounded by the magnificence of the ever changing waters, the cycles of creation and re-creation, stars that appeared and re-appeared in the sky, as they had for endless ages—islanders believed simply in a God that must have planned it so—and that for them was enough.

Even if one overlooked the devout Indians with their temple fires in the night, and the Catholic Spaniards whose priests came sailing upcoast long ago, there was still an assortment of religions, preachers, and devotional services on the islands of yesterday. There were Methodists, Baptists, Episcopalians, and members of the Masonic orders who came to live by the sea.

Islanders generally accepted whoever came bringing a religious message, whether he was an itinerant preacher, a circuit rider (in a sailboat), or someone like Missionary Barnes who later went into the business of accommodating tourists.

With settlements scattered from Point Ybel, Tarpon Bay, and the Gulf Shore to Wulfert, Buck Key and Captiva, it was difficult to communicate, let alone get together. Attending church was often by boat and seas were uncertain. Those who went by horse and wagon traveled over sandy trails through saw grass marshes and a few walked pathways where alligators crawled nearby under the hot sun.

So, early island religious services were held in homes. Later, as little wooden schoolhouses were built, they became churches once a month and the school bell would clang loudly announcing the fact and become lost in the surrounding stillness by the sea.

121

Dressed up to go to church. Carrying flowers for decorations with them, are the Gibsons, taken at the packinghouse for the occasion. Left to right is: Henry, Linnie, Amanta, Roberson, Bessie, Mamie, Clementine, unknown, and Arthur Gibson.—Photo courtesy Pearl Stokes

Reverend George Barnes's church was the earliest known of Anglo-Saxon origin on Sanibel. Reverend George W. Gatewood, who came later, insisted that Missionary Barnes was not "licensed to preach in Florida."[1] Nevertheless, Reverend Barnes's church had a cross up in the sky which he "hoped would elevate the souls of seamen passing by in ships offshore." And, at least one event is known to have taken place there: His granddaughter, Marguerite, was christened by him within the edifice.

This Barnes church blew away in one of the coastal hurricanes, so legend says. Some islanders say it was merely damaged, and eventually torn down to become part of some of the cottages of Casa Ybel—for Barnes was a busy and ambitious man.

When Gatewood came to Florida from Louisville, Kentucky, in 1882, he met Reverend Barnes in Bartow. Later when he came to Sanibel he was surprised to find the missionary had become a homesteader. Gatewood, it was said,

Long before there was a church building on the islands, at Easter, Thanksgiving, Christmas, and other special days, there were services in the little schoolhouses which were decorated with loving care—and to which all were welcome. Above is Easter 1897 in the Sanibel schoolhouse.—Photo courtesy Clarence Rutland

123

long before he was licensed to preach had been "about the Lord's work" among the Everglades Indians.

On Sanibel he operated a tiny store, sold a little real estate, and in 1900, was Census taker for the U.S. Government. Thus he eked out a living until he was ordained in 1900. Thereafter, he held the status of minister in the Florida Conference of the Methodist Church and came monthly from Punta Gorda to Sanibel and Captiva as part of his regular preaching circuit.

It was Reverend Gatewood who married Bessie Gibson and Jesse Carter on the old Carter homestead. He made a special steamer trip down Bay and Sound for the occasion. After the wedding ceremony there was a big dance for "anyone who had a mind to stay" for guests had come by boat, wagon, and on foot.

The preacher traveled sometimes on a Cuban pony over land, often he "hitched a ride" in a sailboat with a fisherman, and occasionally he walked on his Methodist way from island to island, preaching to isolated families wherever he found

There was still no church building on the islands in 1915, when this photograph was made of the Sanibel Sunday School, with teacher Mildred Page in center. In the extreme right, front row, is Ernest Bailey, the fifth from the left is Lyman Frank. In the second row, the second man is Arthur (or Hugh) Thornton. At the extreme left, top row, is Clarence Rutland. Others remain unidentified.— Photo courtesy Clarence Rutland

them. When he grew very old, he wrote several small books, like *Coconut Coasts* and *Ox-cart Days to Airplanes,* which were published in Punta Gorda and told interesting tales of these journeys.

Another Sanibel preacher was Father Rudolph Stahley. He held weekly Episcopalian services at The Matthews on the Gulf. The Nutt family was "usually creditably represented in his congregation."[2] (Services were held in the central room of an inn or boardinghouse in season for tourists seldom strayed far from the place where they had taken up residence for the season.)

According to island legend, Reverend Stahley, too, had "worked" among the Indians—long before there was a recognized mission among them. He was said to have had a "green thumb . . . could make anything grow." And he had one peculiarity no one ever forgot: When he went into the water—for any reason whatever—he kept his old, battered, black hat firmly on his head.

When he died, Reverend Stahley left a will remembering a long list of beloved friends. But that was all he had to leave for he had been penniless for years.

Religion on Buck Key was accomplished by the Knowles family having services in their home. Not to be outdone, Captain Ormsby reported a good Sunday school there in April 1907, and in 1908, Mrs. Hattie Brainard announced the need for a Sunday school. She requested all interested to meet at the school and offered an added attraction in the form of a debate on the subject: "City Versus Country Life."

In time the Captiva Community Church (see page 118) was the mecca for settlers from Wulfert and all Captiva—though Captiva was twice as long as it is now.

In the early days the Bryants arrived by boat. When the wind would begin to rise, the grown-ups would tell the children to "sit down hard," and they would pipe up: "I is sittin' hard."

Captain J. J. Dinkins and his wife came from Wulfert. She was a huge three-hundred-pound woman, seeming to overflow the little sailboat as it approached the landing.

In later time, the Bryants, Carters, and others came over-land by wagon.

All the while, because churchgoers had to come so far and return home before night (provided wind and tides were right), there were splendid basket dinners held outdoors on the grounds of the little school-church house by the sea.

Preachers came and went but teachers and parents remained, so did holidays. Thanksgiving meant a program at the schoolhouses and at Wulfert, a big dinner out of doors in the shady grove on the banks of Bowen's Bayou.

In 1904, the Sanibel school's Thanksgiving observance was recorded as "outstanding."

The walls were decorated with "palms leaves and festoons of tangerines, intertwined with chains of corn—the grain being used as beads. The table was decorated with grapefruit, chrysanthemums, and a pyramid of pumpkins and golden-rod."

There was a big hamper filled with many varieties of vegetables grown on the islands through the seasons. Pupils sang and gave recitations—all appropriate of the season—and a special talk by a winter visitor on the islands "made Thanksgiving complete."

Early Christmases were not observed so much as a religious time as later ones. Around Point Ybel, where the Shanahans and Rutlands had combined and became a family of thirteen children, not much was expected in the way of presents.

As the children grew up, they cut a myrtle tree which they trimmed with seashells and popcorn. An orange, an apple or two was appreciated. If they "got anything" (meaning gifts) they made them. But there was always plenty to eat, always plenty of fun.

Tourists staying at the two hotels on the Gulf, Casa Ybel and The Matthews had no shopping problem: They did not shop. For the holidays they made fancy gifts by hand, surprising each other. The hotel owners had Christmas trees for them and special treats for whoever was there.

When farming prospered in the Wulfert area and around Tarpon Bay, men sometimes sailed to Key West for a barrel of Christmas good things. Art Gibson remembers hanging up a Christmas stocking. Boys, he said, received pocket knives and girls a small doll. For the most part, Christmas meant good food and plenty of it for all.

Belton Johnson, on Captiva, in 1968, could still recall with pleasure the gift of an apple, a banana, or an orange in addition to the good food at Christmas.

Up there, the Bryants, father and sons, would bore holes in pine trees and shoot firecrackers in the holes. Later, the trees were cut down for firewood.

There would be a dance at the Bryants' house, but if anyone received a gift it was a surprising joy. There was plenty of singing and sometimes a candy pull at Carters.

Over the islands, there was good fun and satisfaction of living, for the inhabitants had many relatives, neighborly neighbors, few worries, warm sun and trade winds, and food.

There was no doctor or medical care to be had on the islands. No dentist. No nurse. Upriver doctors had no desire to use up long hours necessary to sail to the islands. Even when the Kinzie steamers came, or later after the auto ferries operated—there was no medical service. Homesteaders depended upon themselves.

One of the island legends is that Will Ormsby once got a piece of metal in his eye and became desperate with pain. The surrounding waters—as always, except for the channels—were quite shallow. Will waded through the shallows and swam the channel to the tip of Pine Island, then waded and swam across to Punta Rassa, from which he walked the eighteen miles of sandy cattle trail to Fort Myers to the doctor.

Women having babies were the major problem. Widow Hattie Brainard Gore, who had lost several babies of her own, was an excellent midwife for other women; J. H. Johnson, a successful Captiva farmer was, it was said, a splendid midwife when needed; and one of the gentle Spanish-Indian girls of Sanibel became especially good in the art of tending such women.

Once, when a certain islander was being born, a lady onlooker remarked to the gentle girl and anyone listening: "It's jammed," and she opined it was going to be a difficult birth.

127

The Spanish-Indian girl hushed the woman gently with a quiet: "I'm a doctorin' of him."

And so she was. The baby was born and lived to become a husky man with many descendants living on other islands today.

Islanders took pleasure along with their educational, religious, and health ups and downs, and made the most of all.

While the island soil was rich, sometimes cabbage palms had to be cleared away and neighbors would help neighbors with the task. Around Wulfert, on Buck Key, on Captiva, the settlers would get together. Men cut palms, rolled them into piles, grubbed out or burned roots, set fire to the logs—and made way for more tomato farming.

Afterward, there would be grand basket dinners served by the women, and sometimes even singing and campfires after dark.

They called this laborious work: "Log rollin' parties."

Multitudes of fish swarmed in the waters of Tarpon Bay. For many years, at least twice a year, homesteaders would converge on the Bay, arriving by horse and wagon or horse and carriage, or by boat.

Everybody helped string out huge seines. Then harnessed horses were attached to pull the heavy, fish-filled nets to the shore.

There would be plenty for everyone: enough for salting, drying, smoking, whatever. It was great fun for all involved, even guests from the island hotels sometimes joined in.

Islanders called them: "Horse-drawn fishing parties."

On moonlight nights in early summer, when the sea was restless and alive, great sea turtles lumbered up from the Gulf over the warm, white sands to make nests for future turtle generations. It was turtle turning time.

Hand in hand, young people would sally forth to roam the beaches. When they came upon a track where a female turtle had been, they would cry: "A crawl! A crawl!"

The others would join them and help turn the heavy creature onto its back, and help gather as many as a hundred eggs from the nearby sandy nest.

Turtle eggs were used by some to make custards and bake

128

cakes; other homesteaders thought them too strong in taste. But it was exciting fun and the turtle would mean pickled flippers, meat for steaks, stews, or ground turtle patties. So they called these: "Turtle turning parties."

Sea grapes ripened in the fall. Women and children of the homesteaders then went forth with buckets and baskets and gathered them for they grew everywhere by the sea. They, however, took along lunch and made them picnic days, and later made the fruit into sea grape jelly.

Sweets were never plentiful in the early days, and the Tobe Bryant and Carter families began to raise sugarcane on Captiva. At cane-grinding time, they had a crude mill, around which mules tromped to crush the cane. The juice was put into big kettles, or vats, to boil and become sweet island syrup.

This was candy-making time, called "candy pulls." You took six tablespoons of molasses, seven of water, four of sugar, a quarter pound of butter, and some vanilla. You boiled these ingredients until they were brittle when tested in water to form a ball, then poured into a dripping pan. When the mixture was cool enough to handle, young couples would be given pieces to pull and pull. Then it was cut into pieces and was ready to eat.

So the joys and sorrows, good luck and bad, were shared in the small settlements of the islands. Around 1900 a stranger came to Sanibel and taught some of the young to play a guitar. And ever after there were serenading parties; and at fish fries and picnics, there was yet more music and singing than in the past, for the stringed music blended well with the sounds of trade winds and moving waters.

Map showing route of the Kinzie steamers which carried mail and cargo to and from island landings and bulkheads, upriver to Fort Myers from 1904 until 1936. For a time Kinzies served the northward islands but that ceased when Port South Boca Grande was established on Gasparilla Island.

As the islands prospered, the Kinzie steamers made the above shown route in one day, reaching the upriver port in time for mail and produce to be shipped out on the evening train.

In 1936, Kinzies gave up the mail contract and the Singletons began operating the mail boat *Santiva.* They followed the old route of the Kinzie steamers and carried passengers and cargo in addition to mail.

(Over the years, channels were deepened at Captiva and Wulfert so that wharves replaced bulkheads and people no longer had to row or sail out to the main channel to receive mail and supplies.)

130

Chapter 16

Kinzie steamers, brush brooms, and baseball . . .

The early railroad steamers could not sail in the shallow waters around the islands. They kept to the channels as they sailed down the Sound and through Carlos Bay. Mail and supplies were at first left at "Saint James City" on the tip of Pine Island or at the Light House wharf on Sanibel.

Later the steamers stopped at the wharves of Matthews and Reed on Sanibel and at the bulkheads offshore from Wulfert and Captiva.

The *St. Lucie* was the first big steamer and as prosperity increased on the islands, the *Thomas A. Edison* was added with daily shuttle service between Punta Gorda and Fort Myers via the island landings.

In 1904, the railroad extended its rails overland from Punta Gorda to Fort Myers. The steamer route was cancelled. This would have left the ancient "islands that jutted out into the sea" without transportation or communication, except for the establishment of the Kinzie Line.

The Kinzie brothers, George and Andrew, with another named Eric, had come from Germany with their mother to join their father who had been homesteading up the Caloosa River. At the end of their long journey from Europe, they had arrived upriver to find that their father had died. The sturdy boys went to work to support their mother and in after years became substantial citizens of the mainland.

George and Andrew Kinzie had served as engineer and purser aboard the *St. Lucie* and had obtained master mariner's licenses. So, when the railroad steamers ceased to oper-

131

Coming in for a landing, the steamer *Gladys.* By 1909 she was considered the fastest craft on the Caloosa Hatchee and Carlos Bay. She carried United States mail, passengers and cargo from upriver to island landings and there picked up passengers and vegetables as well as mail for the return trip to the dock at the foot of Jackson Street in Fort Myers. Drays or carriages transported these to the train for shipment or passage to the outside world.

The *Gladys* was a "handsomely equipped steamer with every accommodation for passengers. Her salon was an ideal one. The cook's galley a model of convenience."

ate they began. Starting out with the steamer *Gladys,* they soon had to add the *Success.*

Their steamers stopped at Captiva, Wulfert, and Sanibel as well as "intermediate points" when necessary. Their arrivals, with bells and whistles, were always exciting.

A cluster of homesteaders and settlers would be at each wharf. Small sailboats and rowboats would be going to and fro in the waters. There would be horses and carriages or surreys to meet incoming visitors and transport them overland to the inns on the Gulf. As soon as the steamer docked, mail would be "rushed" ashore to the tiny post offices for distribution.

Around the waiting homesteaders would be boxes and crates of tomatoes, eggplants, radishes, cucumbers, oranges, grapefruit, limes, coconuts, even bunches of bananas, from which arose pungent odors that added curious satisfaction to

The "gallant steamer *Gladys,*" with Captain Andrew Kinzie in command and his hospitable brother, George, assisting, would heave into sight across the waters. Passengers were soon seen stepping aboard to be greeted by the brothers.

The day-long trips were always merry, with fine scenery, good food and friendly passengers. Visitors found the leisurely journey through the water world an enchanted sojourn into a faraway land.—Photo from Clarence Rutland

the scene. Commission merchants, or buyers, would get off the steamer, examine the produce and "dicker" with the farmers. When agreement was reached the crates and boxes were loaded on the steamer.

So the islands lost the railroad steamers but gained the Kinzie Line, and still further developed into a small, unique world all their own.

Except for the "hotels" on the Gulf front and Bay, and the storekeepers, everybody on the islands was raising vegetables. From November to June the crates were shipped from the little wharves via the steamer up to Fort Myers and the railroad.

From Captiva, the Carters and Bryants shipped; from Wulfert, J. J. Dinkins, W. Hope, Frank P. Henderson, Dwight Mason, T. H. Holloway, L. A. Doane, the Gibsons, and others; from Matthews Wharf, Ernest and F. P. Bailey, Harry Bailey, J. E. Morris, W. D. Swint, W. F. Padgett, S. W. Richardson, W. A. McIntyre, J. H. Johnson, R. L. Mitchell, John

The early Kinzie mail boat at dock. Passengers about to board are: third from right, Linnie Gibson; fourth from right, Bessie Gibson (Mrs. Jessie Carter). Inside the boat, in large hat, is Mrs. Clementine Gibson. Fourth from left is Amanta Gibson.

The older gentleman, with what appears to be a stick, is carrying a "mosquito whip," used by early settlers. Such switches, whips, or brushes, were made from the long closed fan of a coconut or cabbage palm. The ribs stripped from the leaves made a fine gadget, as they walked along paths or where to brush away the mosquitoes from face, neck

A favored game among the islanders was baseball. In 1910 there was a championship game. The Sanibel Tomato Pickers that year were picked from Spanish Town, Bokeelia and Saint James as well as from Sanibel and Wulfert. When the great game was over, the islanders had become champion of all the Caloosa Hatchee Valley.

Members of that team, shown above, were: Top row, Ed Hughes, unknown, Frank Padgett, Will Reed, Steele Doyle, John Morris; Bottom row, Sam Woodring, Joe Dowd, unknown, and Pete Jenny.—Photo courtesy Flora Woodring Morris

M. Boring, Rudolph Jenny, J. Atkinson, and Clarence Rutland.

So good was farming on the islands that, in 1910, Frank P. Bailey and J. H. Johnson formed a partnership and set up a rude telephone system. One of the Punta Rassa telegraph cables had been in use for telephoning between Bailey's Store and Matthews Wharf for years.

Now, they began to put in fifty-cent cypress poles, bark still on, to hold telephone wires, with a post-hole digger to make way for the poles. The wire was unrolled from a reel from the back end of a horse-driven buggy. Because there was no interference, only a ground return circuit was needed to operate the system, which had ten to twenty-five subscribers among the hotels and newcomers' homes.

With prosperity, young islanders found time to enjoy wagon jaunts to Clam Bayou on Sanibel (later to become The Mitchell's resort area and back of which became Oster's). There they dug clams, built a fire, threw the freshly gathered clams into the coals and when they opened had a feast.

Occasionally they took the steamer up the Caloosa Hatchee to Fort Myers. There they saw bamboo, palms, and flowers growing inside white-fenced gardens and cattle roaming the dusty streets.

They would shop in the trading stores, at Miss Flossie Hill's, and in McAdow's Music Store. At McAdow's they could purchase Victor Talking Machine records—the latest cakewalks, hymns, and grand opera.

The journey required a day to go, a day to shop, and a day to return, but they made the trip—now and then.

Sometimes on a Sunday people from Fort Myers came to

The *Dixie* off Punta Rassa on a misty day. She was said to be "one of the best ever to ply local waters. A twin-screw steamer she could carry two hundred passengers (if need be), and more than a thousand crates of vegetables."

In 1909, it required three steamers—the *Dixie, Gladys,* and *Success*—to move the tomato and vegetable crops from the bay side of the islands. Shipment now ran into 100,000 crates a season.—Photo from Arthur Schneider

Sanibel with their baseball team to challenge the "Sanibel Tomato Pickers." They would charter the *Uneeda,* or some other steamer. Men, women, and children with the ball players all rode gayly down the river and across the bay to land at Matthews' dock, or later Kinzie's dock bringing baskets of food and parasols with them.

Islanders came down the island by rowboat, sailboat, or horse and wagon. They, too, fetched baskets of food. With the salt-laden breeze sweeping old Point Ybel, the two groups would enjoy a fine picnic, great fun—and then the ball game!

The ball games were played between the Light House and the Gulf in earliest days. Then, the ball diamond was moved to Dixie Beach which was between the Light House and Bailey Road, and there was plenty of room for almost anything.

The memorable year of 1910, the Sanibel Tomato Pickers became champions of baseball in the Caloosa Hatchee Valley!

Earlier that year, Captiva islanders had noted Halley's Comet January 23, Gasparilla islanders to the north saw it again, March 29. During the summer, the islands proudly

John E. Morris, Sanibel Island farmer who later became a county official upriver in Fort Myers. During the 1910 Hurricane, Morris and another settler waded to the Woodring home to "rescue" his fiancee, Flora, who was marooned with her kindred, and carried them to safety.—Photo courtesy Flora Woodring Morris

Interesting advertisement of the Kinzie Brothers as their steamboat line prospered. The "intermediate points" were where a settler in a boat waved the steamer down, or otherwise signaled he wanted to board, between the established
wharves that had come into existence. This ad appeared in the special edition of
the Fort Myers Press, 1909.

acclaimed their baseball team. But in October, a great hurricane swept the coast and its center passed directly over Sanibel.

Native sabal palms went down (an unheard of event) in
that storm and were left lying in one direction as if a tornado
had passed over. For three days howling, screaming winds
battered the lovely, carefree islands. Fragile homes of settlers
rocked on their foundations. The waters of San Carlos Bay
swept across to meet the Gulf of Mexico.

At Woodring Point, Mrs. Anna Woodring had gone north
for a visit. Her two brothers had gone up the Bay and the
storm was preventing their return. Flora and her brother's
wife and two children were alone in the storm.

Their house rocked fearfully as the wind rose more and
more violently. The house timbers groaned and creaked as
they held against the great gusts.

Hours passed. Late in the night there came a calm and

Flora and the others looked out a window in wonder. Everything appeared frothing, white. They opened the door to step outside and found it was the sea, roaming its way back over the island into the Bay from which it had been blown.

They slammed the door shut and waited. And waited.

On the second day, Flora's fiance, John E. Morris, and another man came wading to the Woodring house, and with the girls and children escaped to safety on higher ground.

On the third day, Flora's brothers returned with their own fearsome tale. They had been caught in the approaching storm, tied their small sailboat among the water-bound mangroves, and left it to bob in the wild waters like a chip on a turbulent sea.

Every moment they expected to see their little boat go down, as they clung to trees and were beaten by the stinging, wind-driven rain and waters. When one tree to which they clung became loosened and gave way before the wind and waves, they would swim to others and cling there.

On the third day when the hurricane was passing and the waters began to calm, they made their way home expecting to find it gone.

One newcomer to the islands had become frightened and climbed a tree where he remained during the entire three days. When he came down at last, he said he was leaving for good, never to return to this part of the world.

That 1910 storm deposited salt water over much of the land and gardens could not be replanted that year, so farm laborers left to find work elsewhere. The next year, Flora became the bride of John E. Morris and they moved upriver to Fort Myers.

Islanders began to think more of tourists as a business than farming. The sun and warmth remained. Fishing and shelling, they said, were better than ever.

Part III

GAY SLOW FERRIES VS. MAINLAND BRIDGE

Theodore Roosevelt, former President of the United States, and scientist Russell J. Coles at Captiva, *circa* 1913. They captured one *manta ray* (devilfish) with a twenty-five foot spread which they hauled ashore so that Roosevelt could kneel upon it in a pose for pictures. When he arose, his knees were thoroughly blackened by the inky substances the ray exuded. The creature was mounted and sent to the Museum of Natural History, New York, for display.

The above autographed photograph was received from these men by Margaret Mickle, a daring young islander, whose tale is told in the accompanying pages.

Chapter 17

Roosevelt, devilfish, and World War I . . .

Devilfish spawned out in the blue Gulf in February. As they busily spawned and fed, with their mouths open, they appeared like strange living waves of sea creatures—astonishing to behold. Men far away became interested in them, as you shall see.

Theodore Roosevelt, ex-president of the United States, retired from politics, had been traveling in Africa, Europe, and England. He was about to depart on a South American expedition, but first he visited Captiva to study devilfish and sharks. With him was Russell J. Coles, a scientist. They intended to prove the big fish were edible and their skins of commercial value.

Roosevelt and Coles had a sort of barge with a house built upon it. They anchored off Captiva as their base of operations and visited Hattie Gore's store and received their mail at the tiny Captiva Post Office.

While in the vicinity, they had shoes made from shark skin and wore them proudly. They persuaded a few curious Captiva folk to try eating shark steaks. But when they tried to persuade them to eat devilfish, none would cooperate.

Also, they received an unusual visit from a small young lady with curiosity, dripping wet.

Young Margaret Mickle, who lived with her family on Captiva in a two-story house (now in the center of Redfish Pass), had a telephone-operator friend in Fort Myers who desperately wanted Roosevelt's autograph. Margaret, who later was known as "Maggie" of local newspaper fame, wanted to oblige her friend and went about it in her own inimitable way.

Sallying forth in a leaky rowboat she headed for the Roosevelt barge. Row as she would, disaster dogged her journey. At length, holding her camera high and dry, she swam the rest of the distance, leaving her boat to sink.

No strangers were allowed aboard the floating Roosevelt-Cole domicile, but as she approached it, the crew, observing her plight, fished her out of the Sound like a drowning kitten.

Clutching her camera, with puddle around her on the deck, she inquired loudly: "Where's Teddy?"

The crew advised her no one could bother him.

She wailed. "All my life I wanted to shake a president's hand, and I'm not about to leave without doing it now!"

The commotion brought Roosevelt to the deck, roaring with laughter. "Anyone who calls me 'Teddy' can see me," said he.

Waving aside the crew, he invited Maggie in for a bite to eat.

Roosevelt made island friends of people like Dr. Walter Turner and others, but he met none so unusual as Maggie. He presented her with a .22 rifle and a picture, autographed by himself and Coles, and later she received letters from both men.

Four years later, in 1917, Roosevelt made another visit to Captiva (as did his son and other relatives down to the present day). Roosevelt Beach and Roosevelt Channel of Captiva were both named for him and appear on old maps.

The publicity attending the ex-president's visit focused attention of world sportsmen on these islands and waters. The brothers, A. W. and Julian Dimock began writing books about the Florida west coast, telling of lazy days and ways among emerald waters and island sea grapes and sapodillas, detailing adventures.

They detailed the sight of waterspouts, the excitement of being towed to sea by an eighteen-foot devilfish with a cavernous mouth that opened three feet in diameter—of harpooning swordfish and sharks.

144

The old Captiva Hotel, taken from the bulkhead in 1915.
On the piling is Paul Ley, who loaned this picture.

Wheeled contraption to move heavy freight and luggage
over the wooden wharf at Captiva. Man is Lovick Holtzen-
dorf, from Arcadia, Florida.—Photo loaned by Paul Ley

145

Ed Ley was a court reporter upriver who owned a boat. His brother, Paul Ley, borrowed it and with friends came to fish in Captiva Pass. They are here shown awaiting the sound of the dinner bell at Captiva Hotel.

Above, left: Ed Ley and Watson Lawler with Hattie Brainard, Gore's little girl, on the porch of the Captiva Hotel, *circa* 1915.

Above, right: Snyder's Open Air School for Boys, Captiva—owned by Clarence E. Snyder of Huron, Michigan, and Chicago. He planned to open it at Punta Rassa but the hotel there burned, so in 1914 he opened classes in Captain Ormsby's Lodge on Buck Key.

In May that year, he purchased the Eyber House on Captiva. There fortunate boys combined study with adventure for three to six months of the school year. The Snyder School operated for about ten years, with ten to forty students. It closed in 1926 "due to illness of the professor," and burned in 1930.—Photos loaned by Paul Ley

146

These books, reviewed in the *New York Sun,* the *New York Tribune* and London's *Pall Mall Gazette,* brought more famous sportsmen to Captiva.

At the same time, upriver village people came sailing downriver to enjoy the excitement of battling deep-sea creatures in the Gulf and of fishing in great passes and back bays.

All were astonished to see mile-long schools of mullet or kingfish and other varieties, passing offshore in the Gulf that made roaring sounds due to their numbers. Visitors to Captiva Island purchased pawpaws, coconuts, string beans, tomatoes—all sorts of vegetables and fruits—at Carter's place. Northern tourists found never ending astonishment in these subtropic waters and islands under the warm sun of midwinter far from the snow and chill of their homelands.

Winter visitors who found their way to Wulfert bought luscious Sanibel tomatoes and other vegetables from the Gibsons. They discovered there were oysters growing on mangrove trees and oyster bars around the Bay. They sailed upriver or across to Pine Island or over to the mainland around Matlacha to hunt.

And while these visiting men went exploring, deep-sea fishing and hunting, their wives remained close to their hotel or cottage and spent endless days strolling along the tide lines, gathering the colorful exquisite seashell treasures that came up from the deep Gulf and the Carib Sea.

These sportsmen and tourists came "for the season" and went away in spring. Islanders seldom went anywhere but stories that the 1910 hurricane had ruined island farming were not quite true. In 1913, the steamer *Success* sailed into Sanibel "with a heavy cargo of fertilizer" consigned to island truckers. In 1914, Sanibel settlers purchased considerable livestock and it was fetched downriver on Kinzie steamers. Mules were in demand for use in truck gardens. Jesse Adkins had Duroc Jersey hogs in pens near his Sanibel abode.

Vegetables, particularly Sanibel tomatoes, continued to be raised although not in the volume of bygone years; and in late season sometimes there were tomatoes found spoiling beside the sandy roadways. Island tomatoes shipped north in

Bay side of Sanibel about 1914. Big building far left is "The Sanibel," operated by Mrs. Lucy Richardson. Next was Captain Reed's home, the post office, then Will Reed's.—Photo from Louise Riddle Waldron

The Sanibel Community Church, known as *The Little Brown Church.* Building began in 1914 and was completed June 20, 1917. It was the first permanent church on the islands. George E. Day, an elderly Englishman, was the first minister.

148

midwinter, moreover, had been the basis for at least one island romance.

A Mr. Buck, founder of Lansing, Michigan, long ago tasted Sanibel tomatoes up north in winter. He inquired of his grocer as to their origin and learned of the islands. To see tomatoes growing in winter, Mr. Buck came to Sanibel and stayed at The Matthews Hotel.

In time, he built a home and came back each winter to enjoy the sun. Still later, his relatives owned and ran the Beach House. And, at last, his granddaughter was married to the great-grandson of Amanta and Clementine Gibson.

Thus is observed the far-reaching effect of Sanibel tomatoes over the years.

Farming continued until World War I (1917-1918). Then, the steamers, most of the crews, and farm help, as well as potash used for fertilizer—all went to war. After that, farming never resumed.

The islanders still held out-of-door oyster roasts over at Dwight's Settlement (Wulfert) and visited Stoke's Hammock on the Bay. Important visitors were charmed when they went "around the island" to the Nutt home, Gray Gables, where they were entertained with coffee, and where there was sometimes still, a dance.

From The Matthews, two ponies attached to a cart would trot along the shore to Point Ybel with guests who would catch fish in Carlos Pass for luncheon. After a fine picnic, they were driven back in the sunset along the shore to the inn.

Until World War I took the island young men away to war, the old custom of baseball games continued. So did sailing parties. The young gathered at Riddle's on Tarpon Bay and sang sentimental songs. And all the while there was the church organ or piano on Sundays, and stringed music wherever the groups came together for dancing and frolics.

Religion and education, though separate, continued equal in importance. New Year's Day 1911 was celebrated by the organization of a Sunday school with fifty-two members (see photo p. 124). In December 1913, Mrs. Richardson, Mr. Riddle, and Mr. Johnson were appointed to secure an organ for

149

the Sunday school, and shortly, there it was in the schoolhouse ready for use. In March 1915, a "protracted meeting" was held in the schoolhouse "near Johnson Corners"; twenty-two were "converted," and were *equally divided* between Methodists and Baptists.

About 1917, Reverend Owens became teacher at the Captiva school, and preached there monthly. He and his students patriotically changed the school grounds into a wartime vegetable garden.

Prior to this, when the United States declared war on Germany, Reverend Owens led the school in celebration. The building was decorated with flags, palms, and flowers, a social half hour with singing and entertainment, a speaking contest—and ninety dollars was collected for Liberty Loans by the pupils.

When the school closed, May 1919, Captain Smith's daughter, who had been in France as a Red Cross nurse, was present and "gave a talk, illustrated with pictures, and ice cream was served."

No less patriotic was Sanibel. In May 1918, to the "great credit of teachers and pupils," there was a "Flag Drill" in the beautifully decorated schoolroom, which was "gratifying" to the loyal audience that overflowed the school.

Moreover, in June, the Sanibel "Civic Club" met at Gray Gables to discuss with the Nutt girls the coming school year and the "difficulty of intensive child culture, etc.," under "war conditions and demands."

What war conditions and demands were made upon these far away islands was not disclosed. But island education and culture somehow carried on.

In 1914, at the beginning of World War I in Europe, plans were laid to build the first island community church on Sanibel. It was not to be completed until 1917, after the United States had entered that war.

The site for it was given by the Robert Mitchells, who owned a grapefruit and lime grove they had purchased from the Dunlap family. To pay for building materials, island women raised money by having "food sales" during the tourist seasons. All labor was donated by the men of the island.

Building materials were ordered and hauled from the Wulfert boat landing in a mule-drawn wagon by Clarence Rutland and John Bruaw.

Ernest Bailey donated creosote and linseed oil for use in preserving the lumber. This caused the boards to turn brown and gave the new church its favorite name: *The Little Brown Church.*

Sometimes the ministers were Episcopal, sometimes Methodist, again Presbyterian. People of all faiths were welcome to attend and worship together.

Existing church records from 1914 to 1922 show family names of Turner, Shanahan, Mitchell, Seigler, Williams, Caxambas, Swint, Frank, Adkins, Page, Woodring, Daniels, Janes, Rutland, Fletcher, Riddle, Reed, Wiles, Nelson, and Richardson. There were, it was said, "undoubtedly many other names, like those of the Nutt family, that were never written into the records who contributed to its final success.

In this first community church, the first Christmas has remained forever beautiful in the memory of all who were there: perhaps because it had been so long in the building, perhaps because it was in the time of a world at war and the islands seemed a sanctuary of peace.

Frank Bailey read the Christmas Story. There was carol singing by the congregation which was called "Vesper Services." After services, all went to the schoolhouse which had already been decorated. There were Christmas gifts for all island children, native and tourist, including the few Negro children that had come to the island. Everybody was welcome and they all sang carols again, together.

In recent time, Miss Sidney Baldwin, of the Peoria, Illinois, *Star* recalled that Christmas long ago.

"Casa Ybel," she wrote, "had one old seven passenger automobile that only one of the servants could run. He loaded it up on Christmas Eve and took us all to the church where the island children sang Christmas songs. . . . The air was soft and mild. . . . The door of the church stood open and . . . against the screen of the back door a tangle of morning glories . . . clung to the mesh—like a design on a stained glass window. . . ."

There was, some thought, a benediction over the little church that day as it commemorated the birthday of the Man to whom it was dedicated.

And that was the way that it was: Roosevelt, devilfish, a tiny church, and island tomatoes. Each added something to the lore of the islands that people could never forget.

Chapter 18

Blind Pass, Redfish Pass, and a tall tale . . .

From sunset until dawn the variable flashing rays of Sanibel Light were visible to men on land or sea. The oil wick lamp had been replaced by an oil-vapor type in 1912. In 1923 it would be changed again to an acetylene flashing light. Through many of these years, the Shanahans had kept vigil at Point Ybel: Henry, then Eugene, and Henry's stepson, Clarence Rutland.

Henry Shanahan died in 1910. About six years later, his widow, Irene, sought and was granted a "revocable license" to use one acre of the Light House Reservation land and thereon erect a dwelling place. It was called *The Palms* and stood on the Gulf shore near where Jim's Shell Shack is located now on the way to the Light House.

The gay times of the old Light House moved to The Palms. There was a phonograph and round cylinder records there for square dancing, singing, and handclapping as a caller told the young folks what to do or sing. Pearl Shanahan played the piano beautifully, which added to the joys of the island.

As the young folks had grown older they sailed in sloops or rode in wagons or buggies along the sandy trails to the Point. They sang ballads and folk songs like "Molly Darlin'," "Florella," "Kitty Wells," "Kentucky Shore," and "Barbara Allen." There were jigs to dance, and squares, and waltzes.

Across the windswept point by starlight and moonlight came tunes of "Sailors' Hornpipe," "The Devil's Dream," "Cindy," "Turkey-in-the-Straw." In time there came the sound of fiddles and guitars, then the phonograph and piano,

153

and the "stomping" gayety of old and young as they had their day on the islands.

Between Sanibel and Captiva islands was the squirming pass called Ciego or Blind Pass. Its lazy blue waters for centuries had offered swift safe passage to boats escaping rough open Gulf waters to calmer ones of Pine Island Sound. Newfangled cars wanted to cross the Pass to Captiva, however, so in 1918 J. P. Loftin built a bridge for the county commissioners (a second wooden bridge was built some time after 1921).

The early road beyond Blind Pass Bridge—when surveyed under Dr. Turner, road commissioner—extended along the Gulf beyond what is now Redfish Pass to what is now Upper Captiva and Captiva Pass. Both sides of the road were planted with Australian pines. On the left going north was a special six-foot-wide strip to allow for walking. Since there were few cars at first, many islanders walked rather than ride a horse or mule.

Clarence Rutland then owned a Model-T Ford and after the first bridge was built across Blind Pass he offered "taxi" service. Drummers (salesmen) from Knight & Wall or Snow & Bryant in Tampa would arrive on the steamer at Sanibel landing to sell to scattered islanders. Rutland would meet them at the landing and taxi them on a jolting ride over Sanibel, stop obligingly along the way, take them on over Blind Pass Bridge and drive them along the shore of Captiva Island (until later when the above road was made) at a cost of $25 for the round trip.

Soon, near Blind Pass, John M. Boring had a farm, a deep well, overhead irrigation, and a vegetable packinghouse. His children, Esther and Mamie, with a few others attended "school" in part of the packinghouse; the teacher lived with the family.

The Ocean Leather Company was the earliest "industry" on Sanibel. January 8, 1919, it obtained a revocable license to erect buildings and wharves on the Light House Reservation on the Bay side for the purpose of preparing porpoise and shark skins to become leather and the meats for food.

For several years there was a windmill, water tank and

154

three buildings beside a boiler at the site. Shark oil, shark skins, and other kindred fish were processed. Then it closed down.

About 1930, a clam dredge worked offshore from Sanibel and clams were cooked and canned at the site for a short period.

At Matthews Wharf and buildings, there was one wharf where the steamer landed with some passengers and freight for Sanibel, with three warehouses and one general store on wooden pilings. There was also a smaller wharf for small boats; a warehouse on the shore at high water mark; a garage on shore; and a small gasoline filling house. The wharves and the small warehouse on the larger wharf were free to the public. The rest of the houses were used by Frank Bailey and his brother, E. R. Bailey, for their storerooms and trade.

During the winter, down from Memphis, Tennessee, came Emmett Brantley and William A. "Mitch" Mitchell. They saw Boring's farm in midwinter as a luscious wonder of tomatoes, eggplants, etc. They saw no icicles on trees, only flowers, grapes (sea grapes?), and sunlight. It appeared like Paradise.

They went away, but shortly after, Mitchell's household furniture arrived in Fort Myers by train to be delivered to the island next day. "Mitch" hired a fishing vessel to sail him and his wife, Stella, to the Captiva bulkhead at once to spend their first night at Hattie Gore's place.

As agreed, the Kinzie steamer *Success* brought the furniture downriver and bay next day and it was unloaded onto the bulkhead and then via smaller boat to shore near the Mitchells' new Blind Pass home. That night it commenced to rain. The Mitchells had to go out in the darkness and drag their belongings inside or cover them somehow. Stella thought: "*Where* has he brought me now?"

However, their sturdy two-story frame house, built in 1910, was pleasant enough next day when the sun came out and they began to rejuvenate the place. They uncrated the player piano and had cheerful music in their island solitude. A rain tank went up outside, a bathroom inside.

Before long, as they began to adjust and the grove was being worked, an island lad helping "Mitch" asked: "Can we
155

have a party now?" Obligingly, "Mitch" replied, "Yes," for he and Stella were entirely innocent as to the wholeheartedness of island hospitality.

Imagine their surprise when the night of the "celebration" arrived and islanders kept coming and coming. From upper Sanibel, from all Captiva, and from hidden places, they came and wished the Mitchells well.

Mitch and Stella had expected only a few guests. They did not have enough lights. They had few refreshments. But no one seemed to mind. Mitch entertained them with the player piano—a new gadget on the islands—and everyone had a good time. Their favorite tune turned out to be "That's How I Lost Him."

The 1921 hurricane came soon afterward. At the time, Mitch had gone upriver to Fort Myers but Mr. and Mrs. Stoner were at home with Stella and Dean. When news reached the islands, Captain Kitchell kindly came over to Blind Pass and showed young Dean how to tie up the boats for safety. The Borings were away but various things were quickly stored in their packing shed for protection.

As Pass waters rose, the Mitchells had to leave the house. Mrs. Stoner decided to somehow take along her fur coat and her father's shotgun; Stella packed silverware and valuables in a suitcase; Mr. Stoner and Dean had a box to lug along.

They made their way through pounding rain to the lime grove and sat on their possessions with quilts over their heads for protection from the elements. Along from somewhere came Lee Trowbridge. He persuaded them all to go to the Wulfert Landing in hope that Mitch might return on the Kinzie mail boat. He did, and Mr. Stoner promptly cried to Mitch: "How in hell did you find this place?"

They all ended up at Captain Dinkins's place where bedraggled Dean Mitchell was stripped of his dripping garments and a shift belonging to three hundred-pound Mrs. Dinkins kindly hung upon him. He was mortified about this for years, but later learned to laugh about it.

When the storm had passed, inventory was taken by the Mitchells. Things stored in Boring's shed had been damaged when the water swept through; papers that had been left there in a desk were unreadable, including their marriage certificate; and for years afterward cases of army bacon and canned foods were found scattered among the trees and bushes.

Stella Mitchell, who came from up Wisconsin way, never did learn to take hurricanes casually as the islanders did. Recently, at age ninety-three, she recalled a time when Dean had to go over to Captiva Island to warn settlers one was coming and insisted that she go to the Light House. When he delivered her there, she climbed the steps and entered. To her amazement, other islanders had already arrived and were making an "island party" of the affair.

While the Mitchells were confronted with their first storm in 1921, something unusual was happening to Captiva. Beyond Carter's homestead, on a narrow neck of land was the unoccupied former home of the Walter F. Mickle family. Walter, being a lawyer, had moved upriver to Fort Myers to practice law. During that storm, the heavy swirling current of Pine Island Sound suddenly swept a new pass across the narrow neck of land into the Gulf of Mexico.

Thereafter, upper Captiva or North Captiva came into being, and Redfish Pass was born.

Before leaving Captiva at about this period of history, there is a tall tale that should be recorded for it has become a legend that tourists accept with openmouthed wonder. To understand, you must know that the little Kinzie steamer left upriver at 6:00 a.m. and reached Captiva, the end of its run, at noon. If a homesteader wanted to get to Fort Myers, he caught this noon steamer, arrived upriver that night, saw the dentist (or anyone else desired) the next day, and returned the third day.

The legend concerns a lad, call him Jim, who owned a Model-T Ford and a toothache. Together these caused him to make history. He made the journey in *one day*—an amazing feat!—and this, they say, is how it was done:

Jim drove his Model-T over Captiva to Blind Pass. There, G. J. Kesson laid planks from shore to his lighter. Jim drove his car over the planks onto the lighter. Kesson piloted the Ford and Jim, with toothache, down Bay to Bailey's dock on

157

Sanibel and unloaded them over long, twenty by twelve-foot planks laid from lighter to shore.

At that time, Bailey's had the only telephone and telegraph on the islands, so Jim telephoned Fort Myers, via Punta Rassa, and begged Dr. Grant, the dentist, to meet him *at the railroad bridge in East Fort Myers.*

Meanwhile, as the steamer *Gladys* arrived, bound for Pine Island, Jim drove his Ford aboard and was sailed over to what was left of Saint-James-on-the-Gulf. From that point, Jim drove as fast as he could over Pine Island and all the other islands necessary—thirty miles or so—to the railroad trestle on the north bank of the Caloosa Hatchee.

At that point, the section boss of the railroad took Jim on his handcar over the river trestle to East Fort Myers where Dr. Grant met them.

The dentist drove Jim to Fort Myers, pulled his tooth, and fetched him back to the railroad. The section boss hauled Jim back across the river. Jim drove his Ford back over the islands to Saint James, where he just managed to meet the *Gladys,* on her return trip, and was loaded aboard.

Back to Sanibel sailed the *Gladys.* At Bailey's, Kesson with the planks helped load Jim and the car onto the lighter again, and they returned to Captiva. Jim, minus his toothache, was back home: The first man to make the journey upriver and back in one day.

It is too good a story not to tell. And yet—even if you accept the erratic timing of the *Gladys'* journeying, the loading and unloading of the Ford onto lighter and steamer, and the time involved—there are questions unanswered:

(1.) To get from Saint James to the railroad was a journey almost thirty miles over primitive trail. There was no bridge over Matlacha Pass until early 1926. It was destroyed that year in a hurricane and reopened in 1927. So, Jim's journey could not have taken place *before 1926.*

(2.) If Jim made the journey after the 1927 bridge was erected over Matlacha and reached the railroad bridge north of the Caloosa Hatchee, one is obliged to wonder why he failed to turn off onto the long, narrow, wooden automobile bridge across the river that had been built since 1923! It was

158

Irene Rutland Shanahan, widow of the first Light House Keeper, with turkeys she raised back of Palm Lodge (The Palms) on the Gulf.

The two-story home of William A. "Mitch" Mitchell and Stella Mitchell at Blind Pass, which is still standing. People, left to right, are: The Emmett Brantleys, Mrs. Brantley's mother (seated), Stella, "Mitch," and Dean Mitchell, March 9, 1921.

The Light House about 1920. The only noticeable change is the sabal palm that has grown higher than the eaves of one dwelling.

The wooden bridge that spanned Blind Pass. Over it Model-T Fords rattled in days gone by, and jolted on over sand or shell road to the tip of Captiva.

Below: A "blue, sulphur bottomed whale," thirty-two feet long, near Ocean Leather Company, Sanibel, 1926. Standing on it are Clarence Rutland, who operated a Model-T taxi service, and others unknown. A few days later it was towed out into the Gulf.—Mitchell photo from Stella Mitchell; all others from Clarence Rutland

159

Man finishing a big swordfish on the beach of Sanibel in the days of the Ocean Leather Company. The "factory" processed shark oil, tanned hides, cooked meat, and made fertilizer.

much nearer to the town and would have obviated the need for the exciting handcar journey, etc.

Still, as a legend, this ranks with the Gasparilla story, and will always be a good island tale for the unwary.

Chapter 19

The first slow ferry to Paradise . . .

About the time The Palms was built, the Kinzie Line obtained a lease from the Light House Board for use of a thirty-foot-wide strip of land across Point Ybel. On the Bay side, they erected a small boat dock, a boathouse, and laid a road across the point of land to the Gulf. After that tourists from upriver could ride to the island and walk across to the shore to gather seashells until the steamer returned in late afternoon.

This was not enough. They wanted to bring their cars with them. In days past, an islander or two had had their cars dismantled and fetched across the Bay via steamer, reassembled them on the islands, and gone rattling over the sandy trails and shores. Then, Kinzies had added a larger steamer and managed to bring one or two cars downriver at the same time. At last they toyed with the idea of an auto ferry but they were not alone. The following notice appeared in the Fort Myers *Press* of April 1925:

"While the ferry service is being considered, the Fort Myers, Sanibel, Captiva Transportation Company will inaugurate a bus service . . . for the purpose of accommodating those desirous of visiting Sanibel Island before the ferry and ferry slips are put into service. Speed boats will meet busses at Punta Rassa and take passengers for Sanibel. Automobiles will be available for trips through the islands. . . ."

Inquiry revealed that a man from Pensacola was back of this proposed "ferry" service. It was to operate to and from Reed's dock near the old post office on the Bay. A "General

The old wharf at Punta Rassa (1924), not to be confused with the ferry dock, which was built separately with hoists to raise and lower a ramp over which automobiles drove onto the ferry. Here a fisherman is getting gas in his boat. Out beyond lay jade green waters and white sands and surf of the islands.—Albert Schneider photo

Left, top: Ferry landing and departing ferry, from coconut grove at Punta Rassa about 1930. It was sometimes necessary to wait for three or four ferries to come and go before you could get your car aboard but it didn't matter. Out yonder was the bright sunlit sea and time seemed of little consequence.

Bottom: Picturesque Punta Rassa Grocery where waiting passengers bought snacks and cool drinks. There were cries of "pot-a-rack! pot-a-rack!" from Captain Leon's guinea hens, and sea gulls and sea swallows flew in the blue sky above wild sabal palms.

162

Sherman" was to be captain, Gerry Lauer, first mate, and the boat's name was to be *Best*.

What happened is not known, but the 1926 hurricane probably played a part in delaying all these plans. Two years later, however, on June 25, 1928, the first small Kinzie ferry, *Best,* began to carry automobiles from Punta Rassa across Carlos Bay to Sanibel.

The *Best* could only carry seven cars and there were only four trips a day—but what trips they were! Early motorists rode cautiously over a ramp onto the ferry and the crew directed cars so the ferry load would be evenly balanced. Then, heavy chains were fastened across bow and stern of the vessel "so cars could not run overboard," and blocks were jammed under car wheels so they would not "roll off into the sea."

After that the ramp was lifted with sounds of clanking chains. The whistle tooted, the ferry backed out, turned into the channel, and nosed her way toward open water.

Sea swallows, like snowflakes, rose above the gray weathered pilings and sea gulls cried in the sunlit blue of the sky.

It was a half-hour ride into timeless time and the sounds of the healing sea. A half hour lost from the world.

Sometimes sunlight on far away mangrove islands made them appear bright green while nearby waters darkened beneath lowering skies. Sometimes there would be a rainbow against a storm cloud. Mostly there were sunlit days, salt breeze, the strange peace of being carried somewhere and having to do nothing about it.

All the while, on channel markers and sandbars there were cormorants, awkward pelicans sailing, flocks of skimmers swooping low over the waters. A porpoise would roll quietly, coming up for air, and go down again into the sea.

It was adventure, away from the perplexities of the outside world. Afar, above sea grape, mangrove, buttonwood, and wild palm jungle on Point Ybel, the iron Light House shaft reared its dark defiance of the years. And the shoreline of the island came closer and closer, until at length the ferry moved leisurely toward the Sanibel landing.

The ferry bell clanged, passengers got back into their cars.

163

Left: Coming aboard the ferry *Best*. Looking shoreward toward the unloading ferry dock on Sanibel in the early 1940's.—Photo from Irving R. Latham

Below: A windy day at the old ferry landing on Sanibel. In the distance is the ferry approaching the dock.—Photo from Irving R. Latham

Above: The *Best* pulling out from Punta Rassa, Sanibel bound. Note the lifeboat. In later years only life preservers were carried. There was never an accident that required the use of either in more than three decades of ferry service.—L. L. Cook photo

164

The boatman threw out lines and made them fast to pilings. The landing ramp was lowered and then ashore cars would roll to seek the treasures of the ageless sea.

Slender Captain Leon Crumpler, of the first Kinzie ferry, had come from a tobacco farm in North Carolina in 1921. He worked on the Kinzie steamer *Dixie* that hauled freight, passengers, and mail among the islands.

On Sanibel, Captain Crumpler met Miss Clyde Riddle, the daughter of George and Allie Clyde Riddle. The Riddles had come after the great freeze upstate and purchased land to farm; later they had a store on Tarpon Bay. They had eight children, so they had milk cows, and raised turkeys and chickens for cash income in fall with which to buy school clothes. On their farm they employed seasonal labor, usually emigrants who came from the North to enjoy the fine winter working and return there in late spring.

During storekeeping years on Sanibel, the Riddles had bought onions and certain vegetables in hundred-pound sacks from coastal sailing schooners that once called at Reed's dock. They also purchased corned beef and roast beef in gallon cans and sausages in crocks (fetched up from the Argentine and other parts of South America), from the International Trading Company over at *Carlos* (now Fort Myers Beach) on *Astillero* (Estero) *Island.*

While working on the steamers, Captain Crumpler fell in love with the Riddle girl. They were married August 23, 1923, and in time had four children. Meanwhile, he worked for and received his master's papers. When the auto ferry service began, he was given full charge, but it meant he had to move to Punta Rassa from which the ferries were to sail.

Captain Leon and his wife hired George Cooper, of Sanibel, to move them across Carlos Bay. Cooper loaded horses, household goods, guinea hens and all, onto his vessel and carried them to the ancient point, where they still lived in 1968.

Occasionally, a nervous passenger showed up to board the ferry. Once, an islander rolled aboard, put his car in reverse by mistake, stepped on the gas and shot off backwards over the stern of the ferry. Already on board was a young sturdy

165

fellow who promptly volunteered to dive down and tie a rope to the submerged car's axle, so it could be hoisted up from the chilly waters below.

There was yet another passenger aboard and he had a bottle of moonshine. He thought the sturdy diver deserved a drink. When the fellow came up for air, the drink was offered—and accepted. After that, the diver seemed unable to get the rope tied below. He kept going down, and coming up—for another drink from the upturned bottle.

After a while, the hitch was made. Then, the ferry pulled the "drowned" car around, from below the ramp to shallow water and a big moving van on the shore attached a long rope and dragged it ashore where it soon dried out and ran as good as ever.

The auto ferry passengers enjoyed the show. The only harm done was that the islander, who owned the car, had had a load of canned goods in it. All the labels washed off during submersion, and when the islander started a meal he had to guess whether he was going to have boiled beans or stewed tomatoes.

As years passed, Captain Crumpler's eyes came to have the look of the bright blue sea in them. He never left a traveler stranded if one accidentally failed to reach the landing by departure time. Nor would he refuse to bring someone across Carlos Bay from Punta Rassa if there was a good reason. Sometimes that meant his making a ferry trip at midnight, or in early dawn. But if he did not think the extra trip was for good reason, he was not a man to be irritated. Ferry rules were ferry rules. The last ferry for the islands sailed at five o'clock, the last ferry sailed from the islands at five-thirty.

The captain, though slight of build, usually managed to handle situations with wry humor. One stormy day, a ferry passenger refused to pay his fare. "I don't think this ferry is going to make it across," said he, "and I'm not going to pay until it does."

In his quiet way, the captain thundered, "I am captain and purser of this ferry. No matter which of us has the money, we'll get across, or we'll go down together."

The passenger meekly paid and the ferry made the crossing.

Another time, an off-duty federal revenue man sped down to Punta Rassa to board the ferry for a holiday on the islands. He was late for he had stopped at a bar along the way to begin his celebration.

As he zoomed toward the landing, the ferry was departing. The revenue man couldn't stop, missed the landing, and shot out across the water. Man and car came down between the landing ramp and departing ferry, and sank.

The ferry was stopped. Captain Crumpler dived overboard, got the car door open so the man could get out and then sent for a wrecker. By the time it arrived, the revenuer was "cold sober" and scared white from his near miss of drowning, and fear that he might lose his job. Somebody notified the sheriff's office. A case was made. The agent (through an attorney) paid a fifty dollar fine, and was never heard from again.

So it went. The ferries made regular runs. People came leisurely and went the same way. Occasionally a newcomer would criticize the ferries for "stopping too soon" when a hurricane was approaching.

He ignored them for experience had taught him when to stop. One early year, island dwellers waited too long to sail to the mainland. The captain had waited for the slow ones and when they sailed to mid-Carlos Bay, he, with passengers aboard, had to buck hurricane wind and tide for two and a half hours, trying to get the *Best* across to the mainland.

He managed to get the passengers safely ashore but by that time the wind had become of gale force. He could not sail his ferry up the Caloosa Hatchee where it might have safely "ridden out" the storm. He had to remain on board, keeping the ferry facing into the wind and, "with the Lord's help" and hard work, keep it afloat—no matter how high the waves.

Ever after, Captain Leon warned islanders to leave for the mainland well ahead of any approaching storm and set a time limit for his final trip. Anyone who failed to heed his warnings, was obliged to remain on the islands until the storm had come and passed, and the ferries started to run again.

Periwinkle Drive of sand and shell, about fifteen feet wide, in the early days of auto travel. About 1930.—Sanibel Packing Company photo

It was still a water world around the islands. What roads there were were mostly sandy ruts.

From Matthews Wharf there was a fifteen-foot-wide "hard-surfaced" road of sand and shell along the fringe of the Light House Reservation to the forks near where Bailey's Service Station is today. Westward from the forks, a fairly good road went through the balance of Sanibel, over the bridge at Blind Pass and on to Captiva. This was used by autos, trucks, and pedestrians heading to and from the wharf for steamer service to and from the mainland.

Northwest from this wharf over a winding sand and shell road about twelve feet wide along the bay, folks reached the Sanibel Post Office on the bay.

Throughout most of the years, the Light House Board had refused to allow roads built on the Reservation. But, just as the unauthorized wharf of Matthews had materialized, so did several routes of travel come into being in various directions.

From the forks of the road east, there was a sand and shell single auto trail used by those bound for the Light House, to Mrs. Henry Shanahan's, by lessees of the reservation en route from Matthews Wharf and by occasional tourists bound for the Light House and the sunswept white sands of Point Ybel.

To Ocean Leather Company, a single, seldom used auto trail meandered for years from the fork of the road.

From the fork to the south beach was a sand and shell single auto trail used for pleasure trips and from Kinzie Brothers' dock to the south beach went a sand and shell path,

168

On Captiva, in early auto days, you drove out onto the dock for gas. Approaching Andy's Dock on land the only two autos on the island at one time managed to run together and demolish each other, which amused the islanders immensely.—Photo from Andy Rosse

used for pleasure trips by people who came on foot on the ferry to shell on the outer beach.

For a time both steamers and ferries operated. The Tarpon Bay Road and the twisting road to Casa Ybel and The Matthews was a sandy trace. It was said a stranger could turn his auto beachward, take his hands off the wheel, and the sandy ruts would keep the car in line as though guided by unseen hands. But then there were cool, salt-laden waters rolling out there in the sun.

And along the Gulf shore from Casa Ybel to the Matthews and the Nutt home, there was a shady roadway to drive horse, mule drawn carriage, wagon, or an adventuring car, where foaming surf rolled near and translucent waves broke beyond.

On Captiva, the road was unpaved but ran several feet above the sandy shore and was flanked by tropical vegetation and palm shade. Over on the Sound side a road went to Andy's Dock.

In very early days of auto "traffic" on that island something happened that islanders are laughing about yet.

A fellow named C. B. Randall had a 1924, four-door, Buick sedan. Another fellow, Henry Rhodes, who worked for C. B. Chadwick, had a Model-T Ford. One summer, when theirs were the only cars left on Captiva, one of these men forgot something and headed his car back toward the "store" on Andy's Dock. The other fellow was heading for the same place, unseen, approaching the bend of the road.

They hit each other as they sped toward the dock and store, at a place where the two trails met. Both cars were wrecked.

The hilarious irony was that there was a whole island of space, yet two cars met at the same point at the same time when nobody was in a hurry for anything. The incident has been retold over the years by the tale tellers at Andy's Dock with delightful embellishments.

Back on Sanibel, during the late 1920's, a goodly portion of the Light House Reservation land was sold. In the 1930's under WPA, main roads of the islands were paved: Captiva first, later Sanibel.

Meanwhile, there were the open waters of Gulf, Bay, and Sound, and on windy days, salt spray, and always the sweet trade winds—as the ferries made their way across Carlos Bay.

Chapter 20

Respite from tomorrow . . .

The Depression years on the islands held the future in suspension. Though doldrums gripped the United States and world, the islands were at peace. An unknown poet of that time wrote: "On these lone isles the tumult of the town is all forgot. . . ." Winter visitors and travelers who somehow found their way across Carlos Bay on the ferries came back year after year.

Someone suddenly "discovered" that Sanibel—because it lay east and west instead of north and south in the Gulf like other islands—lay open to currents from Yucatan and the Caribbean Sea. That was why such gorgeous seashells were cast ashore there. In fact, it was said, that except for the Australian Barrier Reef and a lonely Southwest Pacific island, Sanibel was "the finest shelling beach in the world!"

Moreover, gathering of seashells and collecting rare specimens around the islands cost almost nothing.

From these a splendid mad pastime of the Depression was born. People left their cars at Punta Rassa and rode the ferry on foot to walk across Point Ybel and shell all day. People shared one car with a group of folks, splitting expenses, and crossed on the ferry to picnic all day and gather seashells under the sun.

You might meet Edna St. Vincent Millay, world-famous poet, seeking inspiration and seashells on the silver sands; or Mrs. R. V. Perry, physician and scientist of Asheville, North Carolina, adding to her collection and planning a poem of her own about shells of the sea.

Clara Stran, a French woman speaking broken English, a

unique soul with a philosophy all her own, who walked barefoot, her bushy hair outstanding, set up a small shop where she made seashell novelties and sold curios of the shore.

Lillias Cockerill became fascinated and sold rare shells to collectors around the world. Once, she received a letter addressed to her from Asia, which read: *"Mrs. Lillias Cockerill, Sanibel, Wherever that is, U.S.A."*

Out of all this gay madness, the Sanibel Seashell Show was born. Although there had been exhibits and fairs long before, the shows reached a peak in the 1930's.

In the 1880's and 1890's, a few tourists isolated along the Gulf shore habitations began gathering seashells for pleasure. While their men fished in passes for devilfish and sharks, the women wandered the shore as children gathered colorful pebbles, and picked up seashells from the shore.

By about 1900, such visitors at Casa Ybel and The Matthews had begun to arrange seashells into patterns. Their hosts had tables set up outside guests' rooms on which to display their treasures. Then, the inns allowed the displays to be shown in glass-covered boxes on tables on the open porches. A timid few began to classify some of them.

Rivalry developed. Shell collectors began to hide their best finds of the season until Shell Day, when they would surprise each other with what they had gathered that season. Guests from The Matthews hurried along the Gulf to Casa Ybel one day to see their guests' shells; another day, guests from Casa Ybel visited The Matthews.

And so it went until 1931, when the Depression caused many Florida fairs to be cancelled. That year, Sanibel Island decided to have one, and to include seashells as one of its attractions.

The Upriver *Press* said: "Mr. Rutland and the Messrs. Bailey put on a fine exhibit of island raised fruits and vegetables. Mrs. Matthews added an exhibit of pioneer and antique furniture. Mrs. Matthews and Mrs. Cockerill entered two big cases of silver, lace, fans, old china and curios from all over the world. Mrs. Hartman had a fine display of islanders' home-cooking, all contributed. There were booths of aprons, shell souvenirs, and rarities. . . .

Flora Woodring Morris, now Mrs. John E. Morris, first white child born on Sanibel island, serene in her thoughts of summer storms, winter "northers", and spring tides of the new and full moon fetching exquisitely patterned colorful seashells to the shores she knew so well.—Photo courtesy of Mrs. John Morris

Two shell enthusiasts of the 1930's in happy solitude walking miles on hard white sands by the Gulf, living with the rhythms of the tides in a vast world of sea and sky and far horizons.—Photo Florida State News Bureau

"The outstanding feature of the Fair," the *Press* concluded, "were the many cases of beautiful, rare and colorful seashells—all of them gathered from the shores of Sanibel and
Captiva or dredged up from the surrounding waters. The displays by Mrs. Willis, Miss De Lacey, Mrs. McKinnon, Mrs.
Matthews and Mrs. Perry alone made the fair worth visiting."

After that 1931 Seashell Fair, one was held each year (except during World War II). The name was changed from
"Fair" to "Show" and exhibits were limited to seashells and
sea life. No entrance fee was charged, but souvenirs, rare
shells, and home cooking were sold to help defray expenses.
For years it was the only Seashell Show in the World!

What shows they were: Heart cockles, rose cockles, angel
wings, Chinese alphabets, Panamas; tops, tulips, shark's eyes
and ladies ears; king's crowns and Scotch bonnets; rare
junonias or "leopard shells"; lion's paws were arranged by
puppy's feet, rose petals with rice shells. All of them had
been cast up by the Gulf, or inhabited the shores, shallows,
sands or mud around the islands.

Almost everyone began to collect and study seashells and
experts appeared on the islands to claim nearly four hundred
species were to be found in the area. Conchologists (who
study shells) and malacologists (who study the life which
creates and lives in the shells), found the islands a treasure
trove of new dimensions.

Rare finds were forwarded to Dr. Jeanne S. Schwengel,
doctor of malacology and conchology, the wife of General
Frank R. Schwengel. An island seashell exhibit won the Sci-
entific Exhibit Award at the 1938 New York World's Fair.

The Sanibel Show grew from a one-day exhibition for islanders and guests, to two days with mainlanders allowed,
then to three days and attention from around the world. Its
dates were set by the Kinzie Ferries, usually in early March.
Time, tide, and phases of the moon all featured in deciding
dates because the ferries were always at the mercy of wind
and sea, and would run continuously in daylight hours on
those dates.

Many travelers reached the early Seashell Shows by riding
a bus or taxi from Fort Myers to Punta Rassa. They crossed

Around the Light House of yesterday there were always pet deer, or raccoons and children. In later years around Palm Lodge on the shoulder of Webb Shanahan, was this monkey, Gigi. Webb, son of Henry, carried mail on the island for thirty-five years. At first he had a horse named "Candy Kid" to carry mail; later, he bought the first little Ford on the island with which to deliver mail for years and years. Gigi died in a hurricane.— Clarence Rutland photo

"Uncle Ernie" or E. R. Bailey, seashells and a small girl, name unknown, have a talk by the clamoring sea. This photo was taken long ago when there were millions of shells on the shore.— Florida State News Bureau

the Bay on the ferry, boarded another bus or taxi on Sanibel and were driven to the island fair.

As ferry service improved, motorists drove down the pot-marked, narrow, shell road through mangrove swamps to Punta Rassa and rode onto the ferry. Later on Shell Show days, larger ferries worked and cars waited at Punta Rassa for their turn in a line that backed up along the shore of Carlos Bay and the open Gulf. When they rode off the ferry at Sanibel, they drove along a double shell roadway under casuarina trees, and coconut and sabal palms, to the Shell Show.

Nearly always, a capacity crowd of mainlanders would sail

175

the mail boat downriver from Fort Myers. From the mailboat landing at Sanibel they would be taxied to the Show, and be returned to the landing for the return trip upriver in the afternoon.

The Kinzie steamers had carried the mail for many years, but in Depression times, they gave up the mail contract to give their entire time to ferry service. The Singletons took over the mail service, following the old route of the Kinzie steamers.

The Singletons had come from the mountain region of

After the Community House was built, shell exhibits were taken there and island residents as well as island guests became exhibitors. For years an artist wearing gold rings in his ears and a piratical costume attended the show, grinning with sheer delight at the incongruity of it all.

Jake and Pearl Stokes began dredging for live sea creatures in 1936 and thereafter tanks of fresh seawater displayed live junonias, angel wings, young octopuses, anemones, a swimming cowfish. Sometimes, pregnant sea horses in a special container gave birth to a whole herd of tiny sea horses which always delighted strangers because the "mama" sea horse was a male.

176

Highlands, North Carolina, in 1914 to homestead in Florida. Later, Ray ran a runboat for a coastwise fish house. Then, the brothers, Ray Singleton, Sr., and Captain C. L. Singleton, had a special boat built for the seventy-five-mile daily run to Pine Island, Sanibel, and Captiva, naming it *Santiva,* a combination of the names of the latter two historic islands. Benches were anchored to the top deck so that islanders and visitors could ride there and see what went on as they cruised downriver.

When they reached Saint James area, they approached a long dock and a small building on pilings at the edge of the channel. There mail, passengers, and freight were put off or taken aboard. People of Saint James rowed or sailed out to get them, while the mail boat backed out into the channel between rotting pilings and old dreams and headed for Sanibel.

For a little while at the old Sanibel wharf there would be bustling activity as newcomers, merchandise, islanders, and mail were carefully debarked or embarked. Sometimes, foot passengers with dark sunglasses, lunches, and sacks for seashells went trudging away over the sand-shell trail that led to the Gulf shore; they would be picked up at the wharf on the return trip in late afternoon.

Then the *Santiva* sailed along the islands, offshore, put off mail at the Captiva mail dock, and tied up near Andy's. Passengers who had just come along for the ride were allowed to eat their own lunches at Andy's. Rude tables and chairs were provided. Andy sold beer and hot coffee. Visitors could see out through open wooden window shutters (if they were open) the ancient islands and waters where Indians, Spaniards, and pirates once sailed. And sometimes fishermen regaled them with tall tales.

Passengers often became "lost" in the peace of the faraway and later came back to stay. At the time, however, they were usually amazed when the *Santiva*'s captain called out "All aboard . . ." and it was time to go. The captain would soon add: "All ashore that's goin' ashore" (which was ridiculous but true to the lore of the sea and islands).

Sunburned, happy seashellers and those who had listened

Under coconut palms were card tables and chairs. There was fragrance of sea lavender, palm blooms, and the salt tang of the nearby sea while visitors happily dined on freshly fried fish and hot hush puppies out-of-doors in the sun.

Nearby, shielded by corrugated iron so the fire would not be blown out by the breeze, were huge black iron kettles and men frying fish in them. Usually these "cooks" wore swim trunks, bandannas around their foreheads, and were barefoot.

178

to the yarns, climbed aboard. The captain started his diesel power plant, took the wheel, and off went the mail boat. It sailed back along the picturesque islands, stopped at Saint James, Sanibel, and on upriver to Fort Myers.

On these daily journeys, the mail boat carried various cargoes from snakes, alligators, and monkeys (for collectors or to humor pet owners) to an organ for the Captiva Community Church and canvas for visiting artists. It would tow small boats (stored upriver for the summer) to winter residents returning in the fall. If someone on Sanibel or Saint James wanted to send a message to someone on Captiva, it was placed in an envelope and handed to the captain who would leave it at the post office there, or at Andy's, to be picked up.

So the mail boat busied itself in a slow fashion that pleased travelers and settlers and the ferries sailed Carlos Bay bringing visitors to the beloved islands. Miss Lettie Nutt at Gray Gables on the Gulf side of Sanibel sometimes entertained at her home with a "coffee." Point Ybel became a mecca for seashell collectors of the world, yet retained its remote quiet charm.

Young people of the "bootleg era" on the mainland found an echo on the islands. That "new generation" would find excitement in driving along the shell road by Carlos Bay to a place near Woodring's Point. There, Sam would meet them with his flashlight and direct them from their parked cars over a one-way bridge to the old home on the shell mounds. Sometimes, on return trips, even following the flashlight beams, someone would fall off the board bridge and cling happily to the mangroves until someone helped him back again.

The same "new generation" from the Gulf front deemed it fashionable to go treasure hunting for pieces-of-eight from pirate days and golden beads and artifacts among the shell mounds of forgotten Indians. They particularly enjoyed all-day trips to spend wondrous days on Kesson's Island off Sanibel, which was reached by crossing over in a small row-boat. On Kesson's Island grew a strange jungle of gumbo-

The mail boat *Santiva* passing Punta Rassa on her way to the outer islands. During the winter season, and during World War II, the top deck was filled with passengers.

The *Santiva* at Captiva dock before passengers boarded and prior to starting the return trip down the sound, bay, and upriver.—Irving R. Latham photo

The end of the run, coming in to port at Fort Myers upriver, after the day's run to the islands.—Photo from Alberta Rawchuck

limbo trees, orchids, and exotic plants, and gaudy tropical tree snails lived on hardwood trees.

Kesson's shack there held amazing "finds" that he had dug from the old mounds—pottery, curious unexplained treasures. They bore out the theories of Frank Cushing, archeologist, that the ancient pile dwellers and mound people had excelled in wood carving, that their arts in painting, as work of primitive people, were of an unusually highly developed character. (Kesson was burned to death and his precious cache of invaluable treasures were thus destroyed.)

During the Depression years, the sheer joy of escape and make-believe on the islands triumphed over uncertainties. There had been theatricals of a sort on Sanibel since homesteading days, as long ago as 1889 when the Nutt girls wrote plays for island children to act out. Nannie Nutt had been especially good at this. Ernest Bailey in later years enjoyed acting so much that in the 1930's he went to California to study at the Pasadena Playhouse. But of all happy island acting, the most hilarious were enjoyed in the years following 1926—after the arrival of Captain R. C. and Lillias Cockerill.

The slender, gray-haired Captain Cockerill (late of the Indian Staff Corps of England) was the author of *Songs of the Gods.* He not only composed music—he read, wrote, and spoke in five languages of India (Arabic, Hebraic, Persian, Hindustani, and Sanskrit) plus some three hundred dialects. His wife, Lillias, a "scatterbrained devil," with a sense of humor, had been on the stage in England. She was petite, graying, and as careless of speech and thought as the captain was precise.

When they trekked south from Canada to Florida and reached Georgia, U.S.A., they stopped at a filling station. The distinguished appearing captain spoke to the filling station attendant in clipped tone of voice: "Will you please ascertain if the differential needs lubricating?"

The young operator stared openmouthed but Lillias grasped the problem. She poked her little head out of the rear car window, jerked a thumb toward the back, and translated. "He means," said she, "see if the rear end needs any oil!"

Once they were settled on Sanibel, the captain busied himself writing plays, songs, and musicales for young and old. Lillias and islanders acted in them, and all had a glorious time.

When there were still oil lamps in the Community House, Lillias Cockerill and Ernest Bailey put on sketches that delighted everyone and helped raise money for the electricity that was to come to the islands someday. Some of these plays were remembered ever after.

One of these was *The Scarecrow and The Lady,* with Katherine (Snooky) Shanahan, very tall and slender, and small Enid Cockerill (now Enid Donohue) as the unique characters that were hilariously funny. Another was a gay sketch about *The Little Shell Lady and her Neptune's Guard of Honor.*

The Census Taker (words and music by Captain Cockerill) was a terrific success. In it Clarence Rutland was Light House keeper; Ernest Bailey, the speaking voice; Pauline Engle and Ida Redd, little sea horses. Frank Bailey and Lillias Cockerill did Shakespearean plays at a Community Hall. Lillias also ran a boardinghouse, with Bailey as one of the lodgers; a French girl was Eleanor Clapp.

Playacting, seashell gathering, treasure hunting—they helped islanders and islands laze through the Depression years. "The Matthews" changed its name to "Island Inn" about mid-Depression days, a few newcomers came to hide away in peace. Aboard the ferry, an infrequent morning fog made the ride an adventure into a veiled water world. And over all was the sound of the sea, the vastness of high skies and far horizons, especially when the sun came through.

Chapter 21

World War II on the islands . . .

The collapse of the Florida boom, the two hurricanes (1926 and 1928), the Depression that had halted the economy of the state had been taken by the islanders with the philosophy and easy humor of far places of the earth. Now World War II had come.

The fine new sixty-five-foot auto ferry, *Islander,* that had been put on the Carlos Bay run in 1939, was requisitioned by the government and by 1942 had become a transport for shuttling of troops far away. The *Best* was all that was left. Instead of ten cars on the *Islander* and seven on the *Best,* throughout the war only the *Best*'s load could be transported. Islanders got together in groups in one car, but seldom went across the bay. Wartime roads were terrible, however, and people had little gas because it was rationed by the government; so were tires. Rosa Bryant and her daughter, Scotia, had a small tearoom near the ferry landing to serve passengers waiting in their cars to board the little ferry.

Curtailment of ferry service and lack of gas and tires, plus bad roads, caused islanders to turn to the *Santiva* for relief. It never failed to arrive, good weather or bad. Folks could ride upriver one day, shop the next, and return the third. Also, the mail-boat folks would make purchases of all kinds and deliver them to the landings.

William Reed, longtime postmaster of Sanibel, gave up in 1943 and Scotia Bryant took his place. Her office was a tiny one, on the ferry landing road, built by the Kinzie Ferry Service.

The mail boat continued to land at Bailey's dock, so Scotia

In wartime, the ten-car capacity ferry *Islander,* in operation only two years, was requisitioned by the government to become a troop transport. The tiny ferry *Best,* at right of wharf, which carried only seven cars, was left alone to shuttle islanders across Carlos Bay as best she could. —W. E. Colton photo

had to walk the shore of the bay to Bailey's and fetch the mail to the new post office. Later, she had a "messenger" who picked it up and walked the shore.

Up the Caloosa Hatchee during the war there was a big gunnery school and an air force base. From these came gunnery crews in planes and bomber planes to practice over the Gulf. They flew day and night, high in the sky, like strange man-o'-war birds. One plane would trail a target on a long streamer, other planes would attack it. Firecracker-like sounds and puffs of smoke (as in wars of the past) sounded strange and alien to the peace of the islands.

A wooden tower was erected by the military about midway of Sanibel. It was about eight by twelve feet in size, well braced and had windows all around. Men reached it by climbing a ladder and entering through a trapdoor. At old Casa Ybel two cottages in the rear were renovated into quarters for the military on duty there. Stationary targets were set up on the beach as targets for planes flying low to shoot at; and sentries were placed on the road back of the Casa to warn the school bus and islanders during target practice.

Once a plane of trainees flew very low where fishermen were at work and began shooting as it came. One fisherman

184

Wartime air view of government dock on the bay and extra buildings among trees.

No aliens were admitted to the United States during the war. One night two Cubans stole a dinghy from their fishing smack offshore and landed on Sanibel. They hid the dinghy and themselves in the marsh beyond Point Ybel. In the morning the captain of the smack reported them to the Coast Guard at the Light House. A manhunt began into the palmetto scrub and swamp beyond the coconut palms of Carlos Bay. The fugitives were captured in an abandoned orange grove not far from Bailey's store.—Photo from U.S. Coast Guard, Miami, Florida

Neat walk and well-trimmed shrubbery of the Light House grounds prior to the 1944 hurricane. The walk led to the government dock on the bay.—National Archives

185

yelled to the other: "That damned fool is going to hit us—get into the end there." Sure enough, the plane flew so low it tore off the end of the boat. Airmen and fishermen ended up in the water. Only the pilot and fishermen lived, the others died.

A few onlookers ashore were petrified at the event, but Charlie Knapp, owner of Casa Ybel, cried: "Anybody trying to rescue them out there?" There was no boat, no oars, they stammered. Charlie picked up some boards to use for a raft and with help swam out and brought fishermen and pilot ashore.

Meanwhile, no campfires were allowed on the beaches at night. Windows of the islands were shrouded in black. Although there was little danger of invasion from Cuba, the War Department in Washington, knowing of the endless invasions of Carlos Bay and Charlotte Harbor, had set up the beach patrols and watches.

As the war continued, young military personnel on patrol would march down the bay and stop off at the tearoom near the post office on the ferry landing road. There, they enjoyed freedom from Sanibel mosquitoes, and soft drinks. They learned just how long it should take to cover that end of the island and soon would depart, cutting across the island to appear at the watch tower at the proper time.

Day and night watches, of about twenty-five men from the Coast Guard, scanned the sky and sea with binoculars. The civilian Light House keepers remained on duty at the Light House but the Coast Guard took over. A house was built for them, back of the regular dwellings. Among men stationed there were Robert (Bob) England and Broward Keene.

In 1944, the Sanibel Light Station was alerted for an approaching hurricane and to watch for distress signals, meaning they should keep watch for sinking ships. The Light keeper warned islanders. Kinzie ferries removed to the mainland all civilians who wished to go.

Meanwhile, Cuban fishing smacks appeared in Carlos Bay, which meant that they, too, knew a big storm was on the way. At the height of the hurricane, wind caused the anchors of the little ships to drag. They were blown ashore, and the keeper and others went out and fetched twenty-one of them to the Light House.

For forty-eight hours or so winds flailed saw grass and sabal palms, and the keeper and his wife bunked and fed the Cubans in addition to the Jake Stokeses, the O. O. Murphys, and others who had come "to ride out the storm." At night, while the big light flashed warning to ships at sea—Latin, Spanish, and old Southern melodies rose from the buildings that crouched stubbornly at its base on old Point Ybel.

Since no one was sure what the Cubans would care to eat, plenty of garlic was put into everything cooked and all seemed to go well. Understanding the language was a problem but the Stokes girl had a Spanish primer along to study, and with this, cautious efforts were made to translate conversation.

One of the Spaniards, during a lull in the storm, tried to describe Cuban cigarettes. "They are very— very—." Frantically he pointed to the flexed muscle of his arm.

"You mean *strong,*" someone asked. He smiled and nodded happily at such comprehension.

While eating, singing, and conversation went on, outside the big water tower was blown down. Waves were carrying everything loose around the grounds in a helter-skelter way that added deafening tumult to the sound of the wind. As water beat against the steps outside, the Light House men went out between wind gusts and pried them away letting them float off so they would not batter the houses.

Yet, when night came again, there was music and laughter, for that was the way of the islands. And when the storm finally abated, the fishing smacks were shoved off from the shore, to go sailing away into the rolling seas. The islanders went home again.

Sometimes a plane would go down in the Gulf and a "crash boat" would zoom out from Matanzas Pass over on *Astillero* (Estero) Island. It would gather up lifeless men, rescue the living, and perhaps salvage the wreckage of the hapless plane.

Bombers and gunners were supposed to wait until they were well out over the Gulf of Mexico before they started

187

shooting. Yet one time a plane began shooting miles away as it passed over Punta Rassa. Some bullets made holes in the roof of Shanahan's home, some splattered the rainwater tank at Rosa Bryant's.

At the time, Rosa was washing her hair. When the bullets hit the roof and rolled into the gutters, she shrugged. "It's too late now."

She finished washing her hair. The planes sailed on, out over the sunlit Gulf. But bullets were found in the trees of Point Ybel for many years afterward.

On the Gulf at Island Inn during the war there were guests and military men. Mrs. Matthews, hostess, now called "Granny," was with her daughter, Charlotta, and others in the big lobby fronting the Gulf. She was sitting in her wheelchair when the '44 Hurricane came.

Winds blew. Waters rose, came across the white sand beach and at last rolled into the lobby. Charlotta and the military tried to persuade Granny to let them wheel her across from the "barracks" that had been built in 1914 to the high-built dining and kitchen area that had been built long before. Granny refused to be taken.

At length, a sullen wave rolled in and its crest almost reached the seat of Granny's wheelchair. Reluctantly then she agreed to go.

Soldiers lifted her, wheelchair and all, and carried her down the steps through the waters, across to the big rear building where they all remained until the storm had spent itself.

Then, when the innocent sun shone down, Charlotta went outside to look at the sand heaps and devastation; and returned weeping to where Granny sat.

Granny snorted. "Stop crying, Charlotta," she commanded like a general ordering troops. "You've seen hurricane damage before. We'll see hurricanes again. But we're alive and this is still the best place in the world. We'll soon have all this damage cleared away—we always have—."

And sure enough, they did.

(Some time later, old though she had become, Granny decided to attend a wedding upstate. Accompanied by Char-

188

During and immediately after World War II there were few cars on the islands. Lonely white roadways led travelers along the seashore. Palms sighed in the trade winds and the surf broke gently on the quiet sands. Lonelier military patrols made nightly rounds, seeking enemies they never found. The beauty of the translucent waters and the romance of these islands caught at their hearts. When the war was over, they often returned to visit, or to remain. —*Hello Stranger* collection

lotta, she set forth. In Fort Myers they boarded the train, Orlando bound. En route, Granny made friends with the conductor. She invited him to the drawing room for cards. They had a wondrous time.

Later, the conductor chided Charlotta: "You shouldn't take so dear an aged one on a jaunt like this. Why we won't arrive until two a.m."

"Sorry, sir," she retorted. "I'm not *taking her.* She's *taking me.*"

That was true enough. Granny arrived bright-eyed and chipper, ready for festivities. Charlotta was worn to a frazzle by the journey.)

If Granny Matthews was tougher than the younger generation, Miss Lettie Nutt, last of the Nutt family, helped win World War II. She went about this in her own inimitable way.

She never forgot that she was an un-reconstructed Rebel, daughter of a Confederate officer, and she was cheering for England, from whence her ancestors had come. But what could she do to help win the war?

As England was bombed, and rebombed, Miss Lettie frantically played records of "White Cliffs of Dover," and "There'll always be an England!" That did not help the war much and her friends grew frantic until somebody finally sat upon the records and stilled the endless repetition.

Miss Lettie was undaunted. Come Easter she decided *not* to buy an "Easter Bonnet" (although she sadly needed one to wear to church, which to a Southern Rebel Episcopalian meant a lot). The money saved, in the amount of five dollars, she forwarded to Winston Churchill, prime minister of England, explaining that she was foregoing a new Easter bonnet to help save England. Furthermore, she requested that her contribution be used toward the building of a "Spitfire," as her share in the war.

Perhaps Miss Lettie no longer realized the cost of a fighting plane. It matters not. So touching was her mite and concern that she received a "Royal Letter" thanking her for both. She was assured that her Easter bonnet money would be used as she had directed. And Miss Lettie passed away content.

Chapter 22

After the war was over . . .

Long before the war, Baynard Kendrick, a Sanibel fishing guide, made himself famous by writing a "murder mystery" story there. In the 1930's, Edna St. Vincent Millay, the famous poet, checked in at The Palms and went beachward to gather seashells of Sanibel, only to turn and see the building going up in flames; in that fire went her manuscript for *Conversation at Midnight.*

Such events focused the eyes of outsiders on these islands. Photographers and writers wrote endlessly of the Tahitian atmosphere and the beauty of the seashells.

On February 22, 1941, the *Saturday Evening Post* published a magnificently illustrated article; *Life Magazine* featured the colorful shells in its February 14, 1949, issue. Between those years, countless other articles appeared.

Not only seashells were the themes. In a column "Home Folks," in the Saint Paul *Pioneer Press,* Paul Light wrote of the "heavenly escape from the world to these islands." He dwelt on the joys of escape to nowhere, the trip across Carlos Bay on the ferry, and described Alice O'Brien's picturesque Captiva home with its big fireplaces and sunny "Florida rooms" and views of Gulf and Sound; and mentioned the tropical beauty of Betty Reeves' island home, and spoke of Dorothy Thompson's, for these women were nationally known.

Another writer wrote about "the Dawn Patrol," which was another unique feature of the islands. It had been started by Whit Ansley, circulation manager of the Fort Myers *News Press* in 1939, and saved twenty-four hours delay in news delivery to the islands. It was operated by Carl Dunn during winter seasons. He became the only known "airborne newspaper-route boy" in the United States, for he would zoom low over the coast and drop early morning papers near hotels and inns below.

World War II interrupted this news service but afterward Charlie Kohler, back from war in 1945, began lifting islanders from the mainland to the islands in his seaplane. Newcomers found it novel and adventurous to land on the sandy shores nearby their island abodes.

When Kohler departed the area, Monroe ("Buddy") Bobst came along and inaugurated Gulf Airways and reestablished the "Dawn Patrol." The latter

Above: Photo by Ernest Hart of the Dawn Patrol dropping a bundle of papers from the sky so that island dwellers in winter might receive the news in time for breakfast.

became a kind of "air-age Toonerville Trolley." It left Page Field runways in Fort Myers carrying from one to three passengers and headed west. In the misty blue dawn over the river and watery wastelands below, above the throb of the motor, Buddy would point out islands in the distance.

Old Sanibel Light House from the air appeared like a toy and sometimes a huge alligator could be seen in the swamps of the interior of the island below. Bundles of newspapers were dropped near Bailey's store among the coconut palms, then the seaplane zoomed over to the grassy strip behind Casa Ybel and delivered a bundle there.

At 'Tween Waters Inn, on Captiva, the seaplane was neatly

landed on the waters of the Sound. It taxied up to the beach where a Negro porter came to take the papers to the inn, then headed for Captiva Lodge and the South Seas Plantation.

There was a guide boat skipper and his dog to greet the plane at the South Seas. The plane had to be jockeyed carefully around until it was within tossing distance of the dog, while the dog barked at so strange a bird in the morning.

From there, the little plane rose up like a bird taking off from the surface of the sea and headed for the other islands of the outer chain along the coast.

Passengers enjoyed seeing wildlife along the flight, for the plane waked the birds in their far-flung rookeries below and they winged upward in huge flocks; there were vast schools of fish in the clear waters of Bay and Sound; the pastel-colored rose or blue skies and waters of the still dawn were never to be forgotten.

And in the wake of the Dawn Patrol, newcomers to the islands received and read their morning newspapers, far from the hectic outside world.

In 1946 the ferry *Best* was still operating only six trips daily but by 1947 postwar travelers and island dwellers in winter required more service. A new *Islander* was bought. The *Best* and the *Islander* made nine trips daily in January, February, and March. The other months, one ferry made nine scheduled trips and the second boat was used as needed.

For a time Miss Betty Sears and Miss Evelyn Pearson operated a dining room near the ferry landing on Sanibel. Surrounded outside by sea grapes and sabal palms there was suddenly an outdoor telephone booth. The girls served marvelous food, so that waiting for the ferry became a pleasure.

Driving on to where the ferry road turned onto the old island main road, there was the Seahorse Gift Shop, set up by Joe and Mary Gault—a most unusual little outdoor marketplace with a row of doors that opened back and left the entire front open to the feel and sound of trade winds and sea.

Inside were gifts from exotic places of the world, pencil

193

Top: Entrance to park furnished by Kinzie Ferry Service. The road leads from the ferry landing to the Gulf beyond this sign.

Center: The curiously arranged "doors" were lowered from above to close the Seahorse Gift Shop at night. Posts were of native sabal palms.

Bottom: Later folding doors at entrance to the Seahorse Gift Shop. In time these doors were abandoned for glass and enclosures but even so a tree was allowed to grow inside.— *Hello Stranger* collection

sketches by the noted lithographer Alice Standish Buell, and wood carvings and silver intricacies by artist Joe Gault.

Even before this, and quite a way farther down the island, Andrew Jackson Cole, ex-marine, returned from war. He grew a goatee and called himself "The Old Goat." He raised Sanibel bananas and Sanibel tomatoes, and with "Gert" (his wife, Gertrude), opened the first sandwich and soft-drink "establishment" on the island road.

Jack became president of the Sanibel Pistol Club and had a pistol range adjoining his place. He and Gert won all sorts of pistol trophies—state and national. In the 1950's, he erected

Above Left: Jack Cole, the Old Goat, of Jack's Restaurant, host extra-ordinary to little children and tall-tale teller to writers and newsmen. He gave seashell souvenirs to little folks who adored him. Sometimes he wore a pith helmet with his plaid shirt.

Above Right: Wildlife Refuge sign at old Point Ybel, with small raccoon on top. All the islands were part of the Refuge and no hunting was allowed.

the only "air raid" shelter on the islands so that he and Gert could be certain of surviving any enemy attack.

The road meandered onward. Opposite a tiny beauty shop (where Coconut Restaurant was later established), there was an eagle's nest in a tall red mangrove tree. Sometimes you could see young eagles in the nest against the sky.

At the end of the road was a huge sign directing strangers to various places farther on: right, they went toward Blind Pass and Captiva; left, they followed Tarpon Bay Road to the Gulf, or to Casa Ybel and Island Inn—or to Hier's Cottages where tiny bells from India hung on an elephant's snout out-side the office door (for visitors to ring for service) that were an echo of some far sea.

About midway of this latter road, flocks of white herons or wood ibis would whirl up from the F. P. Bailey Wildlife Refuge. It was an eighty-acre tract of marsh and slough land, leased to the Fish and Wildlife Service to provide year-round

195

Top: F. P. Bailey Wildlife Refuge. A fourteen foot observation tower built in 1952, from which could be seen an extensive view of natural wilderness. Always there were birds, sometimes alligators dozed in the sun. Below: wilderness road into the Refuge. Binoculars, patience and quiet waiting rewarded visitors with interesting sights. Photo blinds were constructed by local Boy Scouts so photographers could obtain natural studies of wild things feeding.—*Hello Stranger* collection

feeding grounds for ducks and other water and migratory fowl.

The Sanibel Wildlife Refuge was first established in 1945 and was unique because although comprising some 12,000 acres, only a small part of it was actually owned by the government. Most of the refuge consisted of individually owned homes, hotels, motels, and businesses. Island wildlife was to be protected mainly through cooperation of the enthusiastic people of the islands.

Postwar growth of the islands caused many to fear there would be no food or fresh water left for the wildlife and birds. So in May 1949, W. D. (Tom) Wood was transferred from the Great White Heron Refuge at Key West to Sanibel and an active program to restore wildlife resources began. Diking was started on the F. P. Bailey tract and the wildlife refuge was patrolled by plane, jeep, and boat. December 2, 1949, the refuge was closed to hunting of migratory birds by presidential proclamation.

Two years later, Jay N. (Ding) Darling, former director of the Fish and Wildlife Service, who had built a home on Captiva, offered to put in a trial artesian well in the Bailey Refuge to raise the water level. This proved so successful that the next year a second well was put down by the Wildlife Service. Wild birds increased in huge flocks.

During the war years on Captiva, and afterward for a few years, the road by the sea was a remote world. The quiet road led through tunnels of greenery—Australian pines, coconut palms, hibiscus bushes—past small houses half hidden away, bleached gray by the tropical sun and salt spray from the open Gulf. Century plants, sea grapes and pink and white periwinkles added picturesqueness to the drive.

Yet for many years, things had been happening (almost unknown locally) to the upper end of Captiva Island.

Away back in 1923, Clarence Bennet Chadwick had come to Captiva for a visit. He was very wealthy, a thirty-second degree Mason, and suffering with a crippling type of arthritis, although he was only forty-six years old. His wife, Rosamond Lee Rouse Chadwick, had been a concert singer with the Chicago Opera Company. Both possessed vivid imaginations and appreciably affected the future of the islands.

On his first visit, Chadwick purchased land on Captiva. Two years later, when he retired, he began planting coconut palms on the old Carter and Bryant homesteads. (Islanders who had homesteaded were growing old by then. They sold to Chadwick and moved away but usually retained lots so that they might always return.) When the 1926 hurricane did so much damage on Sanibel around Wulfert, Chadwick

197

In the 1940's and 1950's, tall Australian pines lined the hard paved road of Captiva along the Gulf making canopies of green against blue skies and beyond the pale green waters reached out to the far horizon . . . to Mexico . . . Yucatan . . . the Carib Sea . . .

The narrowness of Captiva (only one-fourth to one mile wide) made possible surf bathing at the front of the hidden dwellings and boat anchorage at the back.—*Hello Stranger* collection

A pelican wings heavily by, indifferent to the swank Fishermen's Lodge on Captiva. Built in 1910, it burned down in March 1948. Famous people, like John Wanamaker and Edna St. Vincent Millay stayed there at different times in history.—Photo courtesy Andy Rosse

Inside Andy's Dock store in the 1920's. Andy Rosse had been over around Jug Creek at Bokeelia when he met Dessa Dwight and fell in love. In 1924, he took her in his boat to Fort Myers where they were married. By the 1940's Andy owned and was operating the small store and commercial fish house on the Sound at Captiva and catering to stray yachtsmen from the north who came that way.— Photo from Andy Rosse

198

bought up the old Captain J. J. Dinkins lime grove and tropical fruit plantation.

The old Carter home was later incorporated into the office. The old homestead became the "Chadwick Plantation." Tobe Bryant's Bayou became "Chadwick Bayou." The two-story home that Tobe had built late in life, after the children had grown and departed, became Chadwick's "Manor House"; and the small house of Granville Bryant's—where Tobe and his wife had lived and reared their young—was moved nearer to the point at Redfish Pass and was named "The slave quarters."

All of these were, of course, carefully remodeled to fit the imaginative ideas of Rosamond Lee. And when the Bryants' schoolhouse near the shore elsewhere came to be endangered by erosion of the tides, it was moved to the point, also, and remodeled to fit into the new scheme of things.

In time, the Chadwicks owned four hundred acres on Sanibel and Captiva and a hundred and twenty over on Pine Island. The coconut palms of Redfish Pass area and the Chadwick Plantation flourished. Chadwick became an invalid but carried on business from a wheelchair, dictating to stenographers, listening to his foremen (the Chadwicks called them "overseers," carrying out their fantasy of a Southern plantation). He planned to apply for a post office from which to ship his crops.

By then, the Chadwick home had become the main lodge and there were fifteen cottages around the place, which provided accommodations for guests. Famous and wealthy friends and visitors came to visit them. Sometimes they remained to buy land and build homes.

During the war, the Chadwicks entertained airmen lavishly and allowed them to use their yacht for deep-sea fishing. At the end of the war, they sold their "plantation" to the American Hotels Corporation, and the long ago Carter homestead became the "South Seas Plantation" of modern time.

Even before the Chadwicks became part of Captiva in their ambitious way, a Captain F. A. Lane had bought property from old man Binder, one of the early homesteaders. It was

After 1926, C. B. Chadwick planted more and more coconuts in addition to the few already planted by the Carters and Bryants, and others unknown before them. Chadwick had boatloads of young palms fetched in from the Caribbean islands and called his place a "plantation." By the 1940's the whole end of the island had actually become a picturesque coconut plantation that appeared like one in the South Seas. Chadwick died in 1947, but the American Hotels Corporation had bought the place and named it "South Seas on the Sound. Lane had the mangrove jungle cleared and the land filled in. It was known as Lane's Dock.

About three years later, in 1910, with financial help from Dr. Franklin Miles (the Miles Medicine Man), Captain Lane built Fisherman's Lodge which became famous as a resort for touring sport fishermen (the lodge burned in 1948).

In the postwar years, Andy's Dock had become a weathered, easygoing place, with interesting small things inside. In a tall pickle jar, swimming upright and lively, were a couple of six-inch-long seahorses. A live sea urchin, its porcupine-like quills moving slowly but continuously, worked in a dish of seawater on the bar. Back of the bar was a monster hook and a bigger, if that could be, anchor; it was painted red by Andy and labeled "Fishermen's Dreams."

Sometimes there would be murky green waters outside and rain. Little boats would ride fitfully at anchor, tethered to slender poles by long ropes; wet weathered dock, wet handrails. Then, a rainbow would suddenly illumine the surroundings, while the soft sea breeze brought salt tang to the air.

Inside, leisurely folks drank beer and pop, ate sandwiches. Tourist fishermen, in from the morning exploits, would plan to go out again in the cool of the evening. One of them remarked: "Caught a slack tide, an' thet's all I caught—." A small sign on the wall suggested he use "Eager Bait, for fishin', not wishin'." A salesman was trying to sell Andy an advertisement to bring in more business.

"Nope!" said he flatly. *"Too many folks now.* Summer business spoils the pleasure of winter. Used to make a *'git by'*—for years an' years. Now work the year around. Now so miserable I hardly speak to my wife. *Too many people—."*

Chapter 23

Island past meets island future . . .

As far from mainland way of living as stars from the sea was the way of the islands. Where else, for instance, would you find a *Steinway* grand piano and a *Stradivarius* violin playing by the Gulf?

In April 1950 before departing on his last tour, Albert Spalding, world renowned violinist, stood before an open fire in the cypress-paneled music room of his Captiva home. He was tall, straight, almost soldierly but he was dressed in casual gray flannel slacks and jacket, a bright yellow shirt with a blue and white bow tie. At his feet was "Charcoal," his black cocker spaniel. His wife, Mary, was serving tea to their island friends for whom he was about to play.

At the massive Steinway, ready to begin, was Anthony Kooiker, his professional accompanist, and outside there was a muffled sound of surf breaking on the white sand shore.

Then, Spalding drew his bow across the strings of the *Stradivarius.* He played "The Londonderry Air," and the "Jamaican Rhumba," and the lovely "Pastoral" by Frescobaldi.

The island world vibrated with the melodies that came from the low pink ranch-style home among the coconut palms, an island mockingbird outside in a sea grape tree broke into trilling notes mimicking the golden strings of the master's violin.

As such visitors as Spalding attracted attention to the islands, now writers waxed eloquent. "The Tahitis of the Gulf," Merrill Folsom of the *New York Times* called them. Max Hunn, in *All Florida Magazine,* tabbed them "The Get Away From It All Islands."

202

During 1956, *Holiday Magazine* featured Sanibel and a sea-shell worth $2,500. *National Geographic* published sixteen pages of Sanibel's most exotic and colorful shells. *Travel Magazine* printed an article, "An Island Idyll—Sanibel." Even the *Reader's Digest* joined in with a condensation of Ann Lindbergh's book, *Gift from the Sea.*

General J. Leslie Kincaid, president of American Hotels Corporation, which owned the South Seas, built a winter home on Captiva; so did Dr. Louis E. Birch, New York psychiatrist. Colonel Archibald Roosevelt, only living son of "Teddy" Roosevelt, came to visit his mother's cousin, Colonel F. T. Colby at his Captiva home; and John Oster, of Racine, Wisconsin, back from South Africa, and his sons, planned developments.

And J. N. Ding Darling, the noted cartoonist, built himself a unique "Fish House," which was a studio built out in the Sound, reached by wharf and drawbridge. When he wished to

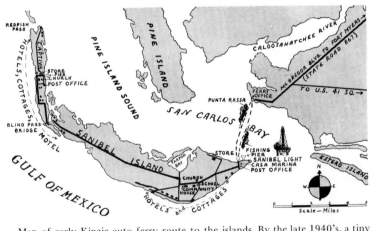

Map of early Kinzie auto ferry route to the islands. By the late 1940's, a tiny restaurant *Casa Marina* was being operated near the Sanibel landing so that the few impatient travelers could while away time as they waited to board a ferry and sail back to their hurrying world. A tiny post office building had been erected nearby.

The greatest asset they had, islanders thought, was the barrier of the waters that surrounded them and kept the rushing outside world from swooping in and out at will.

Slow ferries calmed the spirit, forced mainlanders to slow down and enter another world of sea and sky—*before they reached the islands.*

be let alone, he pulled up his drawbridge and no one could reach him.

Old islanders never gave special service to anyone, however great; all were treated as "just folks," and all came back for more.

To the peace of the islands, its blue-green waters and far high skies, came writer Thornton Wilder, artist Loren Fond, E. White, mystery author. Griffing Bancroft, of Washington, and his wife, Jane Eads, feature writer for Associated Press, came to live where royal poincianas made lace shade in spring.

In one season, at the Island Inn were such notables as Dean Hollister of Cornell; Dean Clench of Harvard; Wilbur Daniel Steele, author; Senator Desmond and wife of New York; Virginia Kirkus, book reviewer; Countess Gizycka from New York; Governor William D. Stratton of Illinois; and Erica Anderson who filmed *Albert Schweitzer's Life in Africa.*

Despite its primitiveness, the islands with their shell-strewn beaches and sabal palm forests and sea grapes had charm and "civilization" began to move in. From about 1953 on abandoned old homesteads, former groves, boom-time subdivisions were in demand. From the ferry landing to the farthest reaches of Captiva, almost twenty miles away, people were "looking." Even Upper Captiva (separated from Captiva in 1921) was sold in part for $250,000.

Poinsettias and hibiscus grew now in dooryards here and there but the fragrance of wild sea lavender and beach grasses still permeated the warm salt air, eagles returned to nests in treetops, and laughing gulls came back from the far north to the sandy shores.

But the strange sounds of hammers and saws came, too, as island businesses and hotels and restaurants readied for the coming of more people. New cottage colonies like *Casa Turguesa* sprang up near The Rocks. Old ones, like Casa Ybel, were sold or refurbished. Charlie Knapp had sold Casa Ybel to the Howard Dayton Hotel Chain in 1946. They had redecorated ten cottages, added a marquee to the main lodge and barbecue pits for frying chicken outdoors for guests, then a few years later (in 1952) they had a yacht basin

Travelers waiting in line for the ferries seldom complained. They looked out from the mainland at the outer islands asleep in the sun and relaxed. They were intrigued by the coconut grove, the pelicans and sea swallows, fishing men and fishing boats of old Punta Rassa.

Early in the morning about six or seven o'clock, before the ferries began running, workmen hired private boats to take them across. Jack's Place, run by Jack and Gert on Periwinkle Drive, served them breakfast, then closed until the tourists arrived on the ferries.—Photo courtesy of Charlotte Kinzie White

dredged on old Tarpon Bay and "laid out" an airstrip behind the Casa, which though only a grassy field brought the air age in.

The new island visitors found deep sleep as they slipped back in time to the rhythm of the sea and soft sighing of trade winds in casuarina trees. They swam in warm translucent waters and walked soft white sands by quiet foam-flecked surf where coconut fronds clattered in the winds like low-talking people.

They knew nothing of what had long gone before them and they, like many others before, were bewitched with the islands and the sea. They gathered seashells, filling their pockets, baskets, and bags with them, and marveled at the endless varieties and colors and patterns.

Teen-agers, wearing gay reds, yellows, rainbow colored sports clothes or swim suits went water-skiing, sunning, fishing. They gathered in small clusters after nightfall on the shore to enjoy oyster roasts, the fragrance of sizzling bacon

205

Rocking chairs . . .   . . . and open porches

After World War II, old Island Inn retained high backed rocking chairs on open porches facing the Gulf. In 1957, a group of a hundred and fifty winter guests who wanted it to remain unchanged, bought the inn from the family that had established it more than half a century before.—*Hello Stranger* collection

or steaks, the aroma of brewing coffee—and sometimes they sang by the Gulf to the tune of modern guitars.

What had begun with World War II, but was held back for half a decade by it, started an inevitable trend in postwar days and by the mid-fifties there seemed to be no turning back.

In April 1941, Lee Electric Cooperative, with money borrowed from Rural Electric Administration had stubbed power lines across Carlos Bay via Pine Island, according to Chief Engineer Allison. Electricity had been needed by the military stationed on the island but approximately sixty-five or seventy islanders began to utilize electricity to replace lamps and private power plants.

The electric lines were strung across the bay with pilings and 110-foot poles jettisoned down and lashed to them. In the 1950's the tall poles were abandoned and an underwater cable used because of the problems caused by coastal winds.

In the 1960's concrete poles began to be used on the islands and plans were for a substation on the islands. The coming of electricity meant power tools could be used for building—and another old way of life gone.

For years the only connection between the islands and the

The new concrete bridge over Blind Pass, opened in 1954, which replaced the old wooden one and met demands for modern auto travel. Looking right from it were the blue waters of the Sound, looking left were the sunlit waters of the Gulf of Mexico.—*Hello Stranger* collection

mainland had been the Western Union line and telephone between Bailey's Store and Punta Rassa, and the Coast Guard Light House keeper's telephone at Point Ybel. In 1949 the Light House became automatic; it was operated electrically from Fort Myers about twenty-five miles up the Caloosa River. June 26, 1950, the Inter County Telephone Company set up a public telephone pay station; it was located at M. A. Beers' house near the ferry landing and post office.

Four years later, November 30, thirty telephones were installed on Sanibel. J. P. Carter Trucking Company had quietly been set up at Point Ybel; it received the first telephone. From there phones were installed down the island, to the Seahorse, at Bailey's, and business places such as Casa Ybel and Island Inn.

Captiva still had no telephones and most of its residents and visitors preferred it that way.

Most of the islanders couldn't have cared less about such goings on. One old-timer said: "When the last ferry leaves the island we have peace. No speeding cars, no noise. No questions to answer. Our own few cars and solitude."

And that was true: When the last ferry cast off from Sanibel dock at 5:30 in the late afternoon, the islands were shut away from the outside world until the next day. There were sighs of relief then. Quiet island peace, never known on the mainland, became a way of life.

Then islanders peacefully followed the tides along the shore, or went night fishing. Some made up little parties for an evening together. Others rested a while, then dressed and

207

went out to dinner, reserved in advance, at one of the special hotel dining rooms.

In the night there would be the call of a loon . . . the sound of surf breaking on the shore. Starlight or moonlight was magic, far from cities of men. Raccoons, upright like little men, snooped in garbage cans until clattering lids caused them to scamper away.

Sometimes on the horizon there would be a light of a passing ship . . . then dark again. . . . And over all was the soft-sighing wind, fragrance of wild flowers, salt tang of the sea . . . and the song of the mockingbirds.

Already old islanders and new islanders had begun to remember yesterday. Through the years homesteaders' families and children of the Light House families had been growing up; they had increased to grandchildren and great-grandchildren. Some had intermarried with other islanders, others with mainlanders and moved to the mainland. Down the road to Punta Rassa in cars and across on the ferry came those from ashore to meet with the islanders at Point Ybel, filled with nostalgia for the past.

Every family brought baskets of fried chicken, "grits," big kettles of "tomato gravy." Men caught fish fresh from the Gulf and cooked them in kettles of grease. Children swam. Everybody gathered seashells and talked about old times.

Through the boom years, through the Depression, they had continued to hold their gay parties on the white sandy shore of old Point Ybel and beneath the high-built dwellings of the Light House keepers where there was still fine shade from the hot sun and a view of the translucent sea-green waters (as they were when Ponce first saw them more than four hundred years before).

But things had changed, the war had come between the old and the new. It wasn't the same. Now somebody else cleaned the fish. Somebody else fetched lard, made hush puppies, made slaw. Coffee bubbled. But too many "friends" and guests came, and not knowing the custom of everyone sharing, they came empty-handed. Once everyone had brought a share and more, now there was never enough.

The last get-togethers were July 4, 1950, and Labor Day

the same year. After that, the hospitable islanders at last gave up their ancient rites and Point Ybel knew them no more.

 Christmas that year, newcomers and old-timers mingled together to make the holidays unforgettable. The island ladies held a pre-Christmas Bazaar at the Community House. Mrs. Sylvia Strong and Mrs. Edna Kearns managed refreshments; Mrs. Harry Dimmick, needlecraft; Mrs. Virginia Way, white elephants; Mrs. Theodosia Brewer, baked goods; Mrs. Esperanza Woodring, fishpond and popcorn; and Mrs. Jean MacVetti, publicity.

At the Negro island school there was a Christmas play. From the Gulf front hotels guests came there to sit on wooden benches and observe it. Among them was a Swiss professor of "International Affairs," a German professor of "Economics," an attache of the Hungarian Embassy, a count who came from one of the French wine families of Europe, and a Russian princess.

At the school for other island children there were decorations as always over the decades. They had a special Nativity program for their parents, and as a "prop" for the event they borrowed a laundry basket from the small new island laundry.

Christmas Eve on Sanibel, carols were sung at the Community Church, where trade winds blew softly to help welcome Christmas to the world of sea and sky. Afterward, everyone continued on to the Community House where Santa Claus presided by a decorated Christmas tree and gave gifts to all children regardless of color or creed. (Mrs. Francis Bailey, Jr., the Matthews Clapps, Milbrey Jenkins, Jo Pickens, Opal Combs, and Eula Rhodes all helped with decorations and wrapping of gifts for Santa.)

On Captiva, at the Chapel by the Sea, islanders sang "Silent Night" and other carols by candlelight around a lighted Christmas tree.

209

At the hotels and cottages up and down the islands the Christmas spirit prevailed. The places were crowded with families taking advantage of holiday school vacations. They had come from as far away as New York and Chicago, making reservations months in advance. As the visitors checked into the hostelries they were told to take their children on to see Santa, for visiting children were included in the festivities and received gifts from Santa, too.

At historic Casa Ybel, where the hosts once served guests eggnog around stoves to be sipped by lamplight while the surf rolled thundering along the shore, now there were pre-Christmas dances and electric lights and still eggnog and the surf still thundering on.

Kay and Bob Montieth, at The Colony, had one huge Christmas tree on the silvery shore in front and a thirty-foot-tall tree by each of their twelve cottages. To keep them from being lonesome at first, all children on arriving were given a bag of Christmas tree trimmings and each group trimmed the tree of its own cottage.

Up at the South Seas Plantation there was a celebration two weeks long. There were pre-Christmas dances. Christmas Eve there was a twelve-foot-high tree out by the waters among the coconut palms to which guests went carrying lighted candles and then joined in singing Christmas carols while they trimmed the Christmas tree.

For New Year's Eve there was a buffet supper, dancing, champagne at midnight at LaPlaya, then on to Casa Ybel on Sanibel for a hilarious breakfast by the Gulf.

There was even a Twelfth Night (Epiphany) celebration, during which the Christmas trees were burned and there was a party and a big cake that had a special present baked in it which someone among the guests received for luck.

That was 1950 but four years later, the islands were growing so that old and new people got together at the Sanibel Community House on November 6, and organized a Sanibel Business Association. Present were Mrs. Lillias Cockerill, Miss Milbrey, Mrs. Christine Jenkins, Miss Ethel Snyder, Mr. and Mrs. Billheimer, Mr. and Mrs. Allen Nave, the Jo Gaults, the Francis Baileys, Mrs. Esperanza Woodring, Dean Mitchell,

After a day on the shore . . . memories of star-fish . . . angel wings . . . sea urchins . . . palm-lace shade . . . and peace of the faraway . . . old and young enjoyed carefree dreams . . .

Frank King, Mrs. O. O. Murphy, the Martin Hiers, the William Reisingers, Jack Cole, Paul Stahlin, James Pickens, Jimmy Jack, Jean MacVettie, and Jack Isert.

At the same time the Parker Mills came back to open their Captiva Island store. Parker had been technical coordinator with the famed Barter Theater in Abingdon, Virginia, in summer. He operated the Captiva store "when he felt like it," and in season sometimes cleared off the store counters and spread wondrous smorgasbords there for visitors on Saturday nights. He had spent the war years in the South Pacific, then with the Red Cross, and in Australia, New Guinea, the Philippines, Japan—and came home to these islands to stay.

About this time, an island bakery opened on Captiva where visitors from both islands were allowed to make their own doughnuts in a special fryer. At the opening, old Hattie Gore's granddaughter, little Dona Wiles, pulled out of a hat the name of Bertha Holstrum, who won a coconut cake freshly baked from island coconuts. You entered the bakery through a tunnel that penetrated a thick sea grape jungle among which were tropical shrubs and orchids.

So it went. In the 1950's, land was bought, sold, exchanged. Newcomers kept coming to enjoy the old ways, to play, to settle down—it was hard to say what might happen next.

Chapter 24

They who sleep with the sea . . .

There had been war, adventure, love and laughter, weddings and births (what else was there to living?) but seldom death in the homesteaders' day for they were mostly young and sturdy with their lives before them. Yet deaths there were and small cemeteries—sometimes only a single grave—appeared over the decades in remote places never seen by strangers.

How many Indians died or were killed and hidden in burial mounds will never be known for treasure hunters have despoiled them for almost a hundred years and shell dealers have sold the material of the mounds, ignoring the bones of the dead. The number of Spaniards who invaded the islands will never be known either, their graves were where they fell.

Descendants of Spaniards and Indians (Spanish-Indians)—often laid coverlets of seashells over graves of loved ones. Big clam shells carefully patterned over a tiny mound told the mute story: that sleeping there lay a child who belonged to the islands and the sea.

Some of the earliest homesteaders' graves are lost. Captain Sam Ellis, the roisterous Englishman who married the Indian girl, according to legend was buried with her somewhere on the island. In truth, she became the wife of another. No one remembers where Sam lies.

Othman Rutland, father of Clarence, husband of Irene who married the Light House keeper, lies buried somewhere on the grounds near Rutland's home; the marker has been lost in time but the grounds are a lovely jungle of palms and flowers.

Woodman of the World headstone, starkly white under the blue island sky, marks the grave of Newton Rutland, 1892-1915. He was a brother of Clarence and son of Irene who married the first Light House Keeper. For a time he carried mail.

Birds sing among wild olive bushes near these two crosses marking the grave of another who once carried mail and his ten-year-old daughter. He was drowned. She was born with a heart defect she failed to outgrow. The child's mother was thought to have been a Cuban. Islanders could not remember.—*Hello Stranger* collection

Two, of a cluster of three, graves of the Reed family who settled on Carlos Bay. Eugene Grant Reed, son, 1868-1889, was drowned soon after arrival. Lucy Reed, wife, 1835-1894, died thirty-seven years before her husband, William H. Reed, who lived to be ninety-one years old.

Oldest homesteaders can recall when these graves were on the old Reed homestead by the Bay and that for years between the graves of son and wife a beautiful pink hibiscus bush was kept perpetually in bloom.—*Hello Stranger* collection

213

Early island graves faced east so that they faced the rising sun, and sometimes burials had to be made where a victim was found. Once after a hurricane, island men went out to see if anyone needed help. They found an aged Cuban seaman, with buzzards over and around his remains. Some hastened home and fetched a blanket; the men rolled the stranger into it and kindly buried him just back from the shore. Then they went on to look after the living.

Under blue sunny skies, where pink periwinkles bloom off to one side among tawny saw grass, is the low shell mound cemetery, called "Sanibel" by some, "The Casa Ybel" by others. Old man Barnes, the ex-missionary, is said to have given this "scope of land" for burial and it is likely that he did. But he may have given it freely and forgotten to register it. In recent years a local story stated that when Charlie Knapp owned Casa Ybel he "gave" the cemetery.

Probably both are correct for there are two adjoining plots and who gave which now matters little. They cover an area of about forty acres and about seventy people lie there in the quiet peace.

Presumably Captain Reed, born in 1830, died in 1921, lies among them. The headstone says so. Yet, the writer, searching among clippings in the Nutt home, found one from the Fort Myers *Press* dated April 21, 1921, that said: ". . . Captain W. H. Reed, 91, 'dropped anchor at last,' and was buried in Penobscot Bay, Maine. Captain Reed was one of the first settlers on Sanibel. He came with his wife and two sons and a little daughter. One son, Grant, a fine youth age 21, drowned soon after they settled on the island. The other son, Wm. S. Reed, has been postmaster of Sanibel for many years. . . ."

A check among remaining descendants failed to disclose when, how or if the captain's body was shipped north. Most old-timers doubt the news story. They say the old gentleman was buried on his homestead by the Bay and if he was later moved they did not know about it.

So, for the moment, it remains a three-way mystery between the homestead, Penobscot, Maine, and the place where the tombstone says he lies, with his wife and son of long ago.

Around Wulfert you may never see the "real cemetery." You may be shown these two "graves" lying shattered in the sun where *Joe Wood* (soapberry) bushes are fragrant and wild sea grapes grow.—A *Hello Stranger* photo

And the warm sun of the islands beats down and the sea winds blow softly among the hidden graves.

Since the tiny settlements were far apart, so were the burial places. Over around Wulfert the grave of old man Bowen of Bowen's Bayou lies alone on the old homestead still.

In the Wulfert area, high on an Indian shell mound, overlooking the Sound, Captain J. J. Dinkins long ago set aside an acre of land (old-timers say a plot one hundred by four hundred feet) for a cemetery. In time the Mason G. Dwights, John Henderson's father, and early settlers were buried there. So was a Mrs. Jones, known as "Carraway" who grew up on Sanibel and died in childbirth but was otherwise unknown. Many other Wulfert homesteaders lie in the Captiva churchyard.

Captain Dinkins never imagined there could be any argument about a cemetery, which was so necessary a part of life and living. Yet in boom years, when Chadwick was planting lime groves at Wulfert, he wanted to dig up the graves of yesterday. Workers on the island refused to help him, so the Wulfert Cemetery remained undisturbed. It still does. And along the slopes below gophers live and raise their kind far from the world outside. There are big strangler figs and sabal palms, and what islanders call "Tracy's love grass" grows.

Up on Captiva, if you wander above the shore, where birds sing among twisted sea grapes and the slow lap of sea-green waves comes up from below, you'll find where many of the

215

early homesteaders came to rest. Take the Doanes of Wulfert: An "infant child" of L. A. and J. A. Doane, "died 1871, August 8th," lies there (but there were neither homesteaders nor cemeteries on Captiva then?); and nearby lies Lewis Austin Doane, born in North Dana, Massachusetts, "near 1844," died May 15, 1921. The headstone of his wife, Jennie, first postmaster at Wulfert, born in Prescott, Massachusetts, 1852, shows no burial date, perhaps because there was no more room for it.

George M. Ormsby (Captain Ormsby *of Buck Key*) lies beneath a monument that says he was born February 15, 1840, and died October 5, 1914.

The George W. Carters are there, too. Very early homesteaders *on Captiva,* they have a lovely resting place on the shell mound above the sea. George W. Carter, born June 5, 1840, died April 1, 1915, lies with Elizabeth F. Carter, wife, who was born April 13, 1845, and died April 23, 1915. Elizabeth had lived only twenty-two days after George died.

Tombstones tell stories, even after the occupants have gone. Consider Julia F. Knowles, wife of H. P., born April 29, 1839, died January 26, 1901: her headstone says "she lived to bless others."

And see the Brainard-Gore-Binder plot (a large one, like Hattie's heart had been) which contains many graves. Her son, Gordon B. Brainard, born June 7, 1887, died April 1, 1912, lies in the plot with a headstone inscribed: "Gone to a better home." Her husband, Herbert Dwight Brainard, born in Canada August 11, 1856, died January 20, 1914, had been struck with a grub hoe in anger by an island laborer. When he died three days later, Hattie arranged for a headstone to say: "At Rest."

Hattie E. Brainard Gore, 1863-1945, lies there, too, and not far away lies Alvin Gore, 1859-1934, the man she married sometime after Brainard's tragic passing. Around Hattie lies her tragic life story.

Not only her first husband and son lay there, and eventually her second husband, but also her children who had died at birth. She, who loved others, could never save her own.

Also in her plot lay William Herbert Binder of Austria,

216

Left: Walk quietly into the Captiva burial ground among gumbo-limbo trees where wild sea grapes and sabal palms vie with red mangroves on the ancient Indian mound where an ancient pathway of shell leads down to the sea.

Right: Scattered and numerous grave stones in the large secluded plot of the Brainard, Gore, Binder families and small stones tell part of Hattie Brainard Gore's tragic story.—*Hello Stranger* photos

born May 2, 1850, died August 26, 1932. He had been a friend since early homestead days. He had been the earliest on Buck Key and on his headstone Hattie arranged to be chiseled: "First homesteader, Captiva Island 1888."

Away from this big plot, in a corner as if to hide from the world, is a small stone, green with age, that bears no name— only the letters "C.S.A."

If you inquire long enough about that lonely grave under the casuarina trees, you will learn that C.S.A. means Confederate States of America. The one who sleeps beneath the moss-grown headstone had been a soldier named Riley who had served in the war. He had come to the islands long ago and stayed with different people who sympathized with his injuries, and the "Lost Cause."

He last lived with the G. W. Carters and was so ill that he sickened and died. Nobody ever found out who he was. He was just an unknown Confederate soldier who had no place to go.

On Sanibel, there is yet another fascinating small private cemetery that was established after the custom of the Old

217

At Gray Gables, within a hundred and fifty yards of the sea, surrounded by lovely flowering shrubs and sheltering island trees, lie widowed Laetitia Nutt, her unwed brother, her three daughters, one daughter's husband, one nurse, and a seeing-eye dog. All had been part of an affectionate and unusual family who lived on Sanibel by the sea.—*Hello Stranger* collection

South when a family burying ground was part of every plantation. It is the last resting place of the Nutt family of Gray Gables and includes that of friends and kin, even the "dog" that had been their friend so long.

Under a tangle of low sea grapes, buttonwood, and flowering bushes the headstones stand, neat, and white, of Mrs. Laetitia Nutt, the sturdy though fragile wife of the Confederate soldier who was buried far away, and of her brother James Keith Ashmore who had served in the Confederate Army.

Of the girls, Miss Cordelia Nutt is remembered by many islanders as "the brightest of them all." She had been a Bible and history scholar; she had told wondrous children's stories which held them spellbound.

"Miss Cordie," they say, founded the U.D.C. (United Daughters of the Confederacy) upriver and saw that it was named in her mother's memory—the Laetitia Ashmore Nutt Chapter No. 1447. Moreover, "Miss Cordie" helped found the first Lee Memorial Hospital and the Jones-Walker Hospital for Negroes in Fort Myers.

When she died, services were held in the Engelhardt Chapel in Fort Myers one afternoon at four o'clock. The next day at

218

ten she was brought aboard the Kinzie steamer and sailed to the island, accompanied by Reverend F. A. Shore, the Episcopal minister and a funeral cortege, and was buried in the private cemetery of Gray Gables.

Mrs. Nannie Nutt Holt and Nelz are there, too. "Miss Nannie, in late life, was married to Nelz Holt who had loved her for years and years but feared to speak of his love."

There, also, lies Nan, or Nanny, who was nurse to "Miss Lettie," last of the Nutt girls when she grew very old. Even "Priscilla," Miss Lettie's seeing-eye German police dog (which was born in Arkansas but lived its life on Sanibel), lies buried with the family. "Priscilla" was named for Mrs. O. O. Murphy, of Sanibel, one of the newer old-timers and a devoted friend to Miss Lettie.

Miss Lettie was the last to go. She is remembered by some old-timers as the "strict schoolteacher" but by older ones for her loyalty to the Confederacy and to England—and for giving up her Easter bonnet to help win World War II.

Now they all lie quietly where birds sing and trade winds blow, "soothed forever by the grand symphony of the ancient Gulf of Mexico."

Each of the tiny island cemeteries contains as many stories as there are graves, and more, for some will never be found.

Some ceremonies were tragic, interesting, or remarkable, according to your viewpoint. The most fascinating may well be those of Sanibel's Captain R. C. Cockerill and Lillias.

The captain, be it recalled, had been "late of the Indian Staff Corps of England." He read, spoke, and wrote in five languages. He had written a small book of poems called *The Songs of the Gods.* He had also composed music for:

BY THE NORTH SEA—DEATH AND SORROW AND SLEEP
By W. L. Courtney
Dedicated to
"Heroes who fell in the Great War"
By
Capt. R. C. Cockerill
201st Overseas Battalion

Well, after twenty-three happy years on Sanibel Island, the tall, distinguished, ex-military man died, October 25, 1948;

and what followed was as unusual as many other events of the far away islands and its people.

Legends report that the captain died during a hurricane and that the once gay Lillias had to "wade out through waters for help; also that she sat by his body all night until dawn, alone." His surviving daughter, Enid Donohue, says "no," that neither story is true, he had seemed well and been out late the afternoon and evening before he passed away.

He had gone to visit the Stokes family, the Bryants, Clarence Rutland, Mrs. Bailey—even Granny Matthews and Charlotta at the Island Inn. Since he could not drive, he had walked from place to place. Afterward islanders said he must have had a premonition of what was to come. It was as if he had spent those hours saying "good-bye," without uttering the words, for the next afternoon in the twilight, he died.

Yet that was not the unusual part, no really, it was what came later.

The captain had lived in the Orient and was familiar with death. It came to all. Also he was used to cremation and wished that to be his end. So, over to the mainland on the ferry went the captain's remains; up to Orlando to the crematory; and back again via the mail boat to Lillias and Enid came his ashes.

This posed a problem. What to do with the captain's ashes? Surely he deserved recognition worthy of his splendid military records, and he belonged to the islands and the sea.

They made contact with the American Legion Post upriver in Fort Myers and it agreed, with the cooperation of Captain Leon and one of the Kinzie ferries, to take charge of funeral services and give the captain a burial at sea: Had not England with the help of Americans saved the world for Democracy? The Americans would champion the British cause!

It was most unusual. Captain Leon was not sure of protocol. Should the British flag be raised to honor a British subject on a United States vessel? or vice versa?

The captain compromised. The casket was covered with the flag of Britain which made a nice background, and from the ferry flagstaff the captain flew the Confederate flag.

The legionnaires stood at attention, as was proper. The flag was dipped to half-mast. Captain Leon's hat flew overboard. But the Stars and Bars flew in honor of the British man of the Indian Staff Corps.

Then, two lads from the high school band upriver, on board for the occasion, played the thrilling notes of "The Last Post," which, it was said, was British taps in English. And, with the two women and a few friends standing by, the ashes of Captain Cockerill were scattered on the ancient waters of Carlos Bay.

That is not quite the end of this story. The rest happened eight years later, after petite, gay Lillias (the former stage star from Britain and Canada wife of Captain Cockerill) died in June 1956.

During her years on the island, in addition to writing, painting and acting in island plays with her husband and islanders, Lillias had became a renowned conchologist; so much so, that once she received a letter from the Eastern World addressed to:

Lillias Cockerill,
Sanibel Island (wherever that is)
U.S.A.

She had requested that when she died she should be cremated and her ashes spread on Carlos Bay to join those of her husband. There would be no American Legion to plan for Lillias for she had no military record. But a Kinzie ferry and Captain Leon were obliging as usual.

Simple services were held upriver at Engelhardt's Chapel and Lillias was taken to Orlando for cremation. When the ashes were returned, Enid and old friends went aboard a special ferry. All sailed out into Carlos Bay in view of the open Gulf. Four porpoises swam and rolled in the sunlit waters in the wake of the boat.

Then the unusual thing happened. To scatter the ashes, the ferry would have to be in a certain position or the wind would scatter the ashes over those on board instead of on the surrounding waters. That afternoon, the wind blew the wrong way, so Captain Leon sailed down the Bay to a position opposite old Point Ybel, in near view of the old Light House. There he turned and sailed back into Carlos Bay.

221

It was nearing sunset. As the ferry turned, the porpoises turned also. Instead of trailing the ferry, they swam in pairs ahead of it—as if they were an escort leading a parade of the sea.

Islanders who were there remember this with a strange awe. They say it was so quiet out there, so strange, so lovely. The twilight reflections, a sudden stillness of the waters, and the porpoises rolling slowly up and going down again in the leisureliness of timeless time.

The ferry paused. The American flag was dipped to half-mast. Leroy Friday, a deckhand, read Lillias' favorite poem, "Crossing the Bar":

> Sunset and evening star
> And one clear call for me
> And may there be no moaning of the bar
> When I put out to sea. . . .

The ashes of gay Lillias from England were scattered over the waters of Carlos Bay to join those of Captain Cockerill, late of the Indian Staff Corps of England, in the historic waters of the world.

So it was on the islands. Here and there, Spaniards, Indians, Spanish-Indians, Cubans, homesteaders, strangers washed ashore in the dim past—known and unknown—lie in peace and even in the waters surrounding. They left a legacy of love and laughter, echoes of happy ways and days, that belong to the islands forever.

Chapter 25

Farewell to waterborne ways . . .

By September 1953, the ancient island past was rapidly meeting the present. All still seemed remote. Inhabitants continued uninhibited, creative, lazily happy, indifferent to time. No one ever thought it would change, but it did.

A landowner and a banker-promoter began planning a bridge across old Carlos Bay. At the same time, the state "donated" a strip of underwater land, 150 feet wide, to the local political unit and it was accepted. None knew why.

That year, the guide magazine, *Hello Stranger!,* warned quietly: *"Down Punta Rassa way, they're completing a new hard-surfaced road as a link to a future Sanibel Island bridge."*

Another developer, over on Pine Island, argued for a bridge, too, but he was a dreamer and few worried that he would be able to link with the outer islands.

Yet the "grapevine" news said that revenue bonds were being worked upon for a bridge and that should have been warning enough.

Once again *Hello Stranger!* reported: *"It looks as if a causeway will yet be erected across old Carlos Bay. For those . . . who scorn greed, it will be a tragedy that the peace of the ancient islands be destroyed. For those who live for financial gain, it may become a bonanza."*

As rumors and tentative beginnings were made to promote the bridge, Kinzie ferries began operating three ferries on regular twenty-minute intervals, starting early in the morning and running far into the night the year around.

At Punta Rassa landing, new ramps were built, a new ferry

office, rest rooms were added and picnic tables appeared among the coconut palms on Carlos Bay. On the Sanibel side a new fishing pier for recreation was erected, the park area on the Gulf was landscaped, there were picnic tables; and Casa Marina Restaurant was remodeled and enlarged.

Two years later, in 1957, four squat trim matronly ferries, including the *Yankee Clipper* and *The Rebel,* plied across the waters from 7:30 a.m. until 5:30 p.m. During the season the four ferries sailed in relays, one every fifteen minutes—five minutes less waiting time per trip.

It was as if the hurrying little boats could somehow hold back the hand of fate that was steadily closing in.

Islanders were not yet alarmed. They poked leisurely on their way, unhurried. Besides if one were in a hurry, he could fly a charter plane across for ten dollars. Also, there was the mail boat from Fort Myers coming daily at $2.48 a round trip. Private craft from upriver cost about the same as plane service. The ferries charged only one dollar for a car and forty-seven cents for passengers.

In 1960, a "feasibility study" was made of the wisdom of a bridge to Sanibel and it, as it was supposed to do, said a bridge would pay its way.

Pay its way? And who wanted it?

By August of that year, many of the islanders were people who had come from many parts of the United States. Like the old-timers, they were happy with things as they were. Also like the old-timers they did not know much about what had gone on before: They thought they had discovered a lost world and wanted it unchanged. Mainland citizenry, who went to the islands, enjoyed the slow ferries or the mail boat.

But the speculator and the banker continued to promote the bridge and great opposition arose.

Old-timers cried out "it would bring an influx of visitors and destroy seclusion." "It would make the islands easily accessible for undesirables." "At present we have no keys for any doors, we have never needed them. A public bridge would destroy our security and force us to add locks to our doors for the first time in the history of the islands."

The newcomers who had now become old-timers begged

224

Flying the Stars and Stripes, the captain looked out through the window of his pilothouse and steered the ferry loads of happy passengers across the waters.—*Hello Stranger* collection

for a referendum on the matter. They were sure mainlanders would join them in defeating the building of the bridge. Signers were: Opal W. Combs, Willis B. Combs, James Jack, Jeane L. Jack, Virginia L. Klotz, Katherine Klotz, J. J. Glough, Blanche J. Glough, James S. Pickens, Robert Stevens, Helen C. Denny, Goldie M. Nave, Fanetta Stahlin, Paul Simonds, Marguerite Simonds.

By February 1953, the all-steel *Yankee Clipper* with 175 hp Caterpillar diesel motor was commissioned. There were three ferries to transport the stream of traffic across Carlos Bay and they made twenty-seven trips a day for about six weeks in mid-winter tourist season. In summer the extra ferries operated on weekends or holidays as needed.

Old islanders were unconcerned with such problems for they did not encourage visitors. Newcomers wanted solitude, seclusion, privacy. These things they had. But strangers kept coming.—L. L. Cook photo

225

Andrew R. Mellody, William MacIntosh, Floyd R. Snook, Maude Snook, B. W. Skates, Claude A. Nave, Dale E. Ballinger, Gerald L. Martin, Isabel M. Reisinger, V. H. MacVettie, D. J. Simon, Allen T. Weeks, Priscilla Murphy, Marshall Tabacchi, Glen A. Rhodes, J. O. Gault, Mary Gault, Robert L. Gault, S. W. Grenetti, and Dorothy S. MacIntosh.

No referendum was called. The bridge progressed and arguments continued. The now fighting-mad old-timers and the new old-timers used every valid excuse to try to prevent or stay the building of the bridge.

Delegations from all the islands rose up in arms. Bird clubs, Audubon societies, the U.S. Wildlife Service, various conservation groups were certain the bridges would hem in the channels and cause erosion, that the earthen causeways would dam up the great floods of water in rainy and hurricane seasons and change the ecology of the ancient water Paradise.

As construction of the bridges went on and on, it became evident that the ferries would soon be doomed and the ways of the waters lost. In March 1963, Captain Crumpler, who had guided the destiny of the boats since service began, had a birthday, his seventy-first. Islanders decided to give him a birthday party, an appreciation celebration, for his years of devotion to duty.

It was held outdoors at long tables on the white sands among the rustling coconut palms of Island Inn. Bill Hamen planned the festivities. Stark Altmaier, from Columbus, Ohio, was master of ceremonies. With them and others at the speaker's table were also the captain's wife, who had been a girl on Sanibel long before, and their daughter, Mrs. Richard Chappelle (whose husband operated one of the ferries). Many were the well-wishers who had come—from North, South, around the world—to pay him tribute and wish him well.

There was a special sadness hovering over those assembled that day for they knew that the end was swiftly approaching for the pleasure of riding the ferries of Carlos Bay. Charlotta Matthews, daughter of "Granny" Matthews (who had been on the island since 1895), reminded the party how the captain had protected the islands and had been a good friend to

In 1957 still another ferry was ordered from Blount Marine Corporation of Warren, Rhode Island. Companion to the *Yankee Clipper,* she was to be called *The Rebel,* and to be powered by a turbo-charged 200 hp Caterpillar diesel engine.

The *Rebel,* true to her name, had trouble up North in Rhode Island—her cradle somehow slipped off the rails at the launching and she was left hanging up about twenty-five feet from shore, her Confederate Flag flapping defiantly in the wind. They towed her into the water then and headed her south for delivery to operate in Carlos Bay between Punta Rassa and the islands.

In August 1957, flag flying, laden with cars and people *The Rebel* churned the waters under cloud-swept sunny skies, heading for Sanibel. Midway across the Bay, she met the *Yankee Clipper* and they saluted each other with toots of their whistles. It became a gay custom thereafter that delighted travelers.—An L. L. Cook photo

all during his thirty-five years of ferry service. Someone else remembered how he had refused to allow intoxicated strangers to cross the Bay.

Another recalled the Depression days when a stranger gathered a truckload of gophers and wanted to board the ferry with them but the captain had turned the man back.

"What will the poorer islanders eat during these hard times if you take those to the mainland?" he thundered in his usual mild but stubborn way.

The tale teller insisted that the stranger had to unload his cargo before he could board the homebound ferry.

Such reminiscences were rife and other tales were told but they did not ask him to affirm or deny or explain.

The captain was not much of a speechmaker but they cheered him lustily when he rose to talk. He had enjoyed the

227

years of bustle ferrying autos and passengers to the islands—
and taking them back to the mainland. He had always appreciated the seclusion of the islands and understood their desire
to keep them that way.

He recalled famous ferry passengers, like Charles A. Lind-
bergh and his pretty bride, the former Ann Morrow, when
they came aboard and crossed the Bay to spend their honey-
moon on Captiva in 1929 and the many times over the years
they had returned because no one bothered them on the
islands and they could be content.

Thomas A. Edison and lanky Henry Ford were ferry-riding
addicts. Edison was hunting rubber sources and came to the
islands to hunt plants, shrubs, and vines which he took back
in his car to work upon in his upriver laboratory.

Somewhat shyly but with pride, he concluded: "We had
and always have had, one motto on the Sanibel ferries, that
is: whatever the weather, whatever the emergency, the ferries
must run—*and we never failed.*"

There were presents from islanders, a birthday cake with a
sailboat on it and lettering: "Best wishes to Captain Leon
from Island Inn." There was a purse from "Leon's friends,
whom he has hauled on the ferry," and a smaller purse from
the Negro children who daily rode the ferry, which was presented by Edmund Gavin, Sr., Edmund Gavin, Jr., and Carl
Jordon.

New arguments arose as fishermen cried the new bridge
would dam up fresh waters of rainy seasons and change
brackish waters that had been vast breeding grounds for fish
for thousands of years; as one or two knowledgeable mainlanders insisted that bridging of channels of Carlos Bay harbor would end possibility of establishing once more the port
of Carlos to which ocean-going liners from New Orleans,
Tampa bound for Havana once came to anchor offshore.

But construction went on and on and the date was set for
the opening of the bridge. The ferries were doomed (the mail
boat would be later), so the Richard and Paul Kearnses sent
out a hundred and fourteen invitations to islanders. On them
were sketches of a Sanibel ferry and weathered pilings near
old Point Ybel and the following greeting:

To you, who on these sister islands dwell
Come gather round we've something we would tell.
We think that on the 26th of May
our farewells to the ferries we should say.

Two ferries Captain Kinzie is donating,
and breakfast we will serve commemorating
our last trip with the men of Leon's crew,
and lasting memories share with all of you.

So, Sunday morn at half past ten,
we'll be awaiting at the ferry slip—
and we will make this farewell gesture
to a way of island living,
ending on that day.

On the designated day, one hundred and twenty island dwellers boarded the *Best* and *The Rebel* at the Sanibel landing. Yachts and smaller private craft, many of them decorated for the occasion, assembled near the landing to help escort the ferries on their last run. Many of these people had lived on the islands since schooner days. Others had come on the railroad steamers, or via Kinzie steamer, or the ferries. All of them loved the ways of the waters that kept the islands separated from the mainland.

Old-timers aboard the ferries were Arthur Gibson, who had come as a boy of twelve; Belton Johnson, whose father had worked for Bailey's raising tomatoes and then become a Captiva homesteader; Clarence Rutland whose widowed mother, Irene Rutland, had long ago married the Light House keeper, Shanahan; Miss Charlotta Matthews, daughter of "Granny" who had founded The Matthews (Island Inn); Mrs. Rosa Bryant who had been married in homesteading days on Captiva by a preacher who had come downriver on a Kinzie steamer; Scotia Bryant, daughter of Rosa, born on the islands; Esperanza Woodring, born on a neighboring island but lived on Sanibel for more than half a century.

Personnel of the ferries aboard were the Ernest Kinzies, Miss Charlotte Kinzie, R. T. Chappelle and family, Captain Leon Crumpler and wife. Also, Captains William Rhodes, L. E. Daniels, Robert Daniels, Harrison Caputo, and J. C. Dison; pursers and deckhands Dick Schaefer, Jack Lowe, Donald

Artist's sketch of the *Rebel*'s last run. Here she is leaving the dock on her sentimental journey for the final trip.—By Eleanor Douglas Clapp

Brest, Hastings Jennings, and Bennie McDowell; traffic checkers Mrs. Loretto I. Lee and Mrs. Dison; office receptionist Mrs. Beryl Lenoch; office manager Mrs. B. J. Holmes; and grounds maintenance man George Rouse; and Ernest Andrew Kinzie, former ferry captain but then stationed in Spain with the U.S. Navy.

The use of the ferries had been donated by the Ernest Kinzies. The buffet breakfast was furnished by the Kearnses and Island Inn. On the breakfast tables were small replicas of the *Best*, first auto ferry to cross San Carlos Bay and little "old lady" of the line.

The laden ferries crossed from Sanibel to Punta Rassa and back again. The *Best* had hoisted the Stars and Stripes, *The Rebel* flew the Stars and Bars, symbol of defiance for the way of life that was passing. When they reached the half-way point of Carlos Bay, they tooted their last valiant salutes to each other—the United States and the Confederacy—in mutual admiration.

As the ferries docked at Sanibel landing for the last time the sentimental guests, some flicking away a tear, sang "For He's a Jolly Good Fellow" to Captain Crumpler. Then they sang "Auld Lang Syne" with quavering voices to the captain, crews, and ferries. At least one guest bitterly thumbed his nose toward the mainland and the outside world that was about to move in.

That afternoon, the new $2,805,081 Sanibel Bridge and causeway was opened with a ribbon cutting and fanfare. Secretary of State Tom Adams gave a dedicatory speech. There were flag-raising ceremonies by the American Legion. Then the cutting of the ribbon.

The day was one of jubilation for a few, the end of a way of life for others. Ironically, Captain Crumpler, operator of the ferries for thirty-five years, was driven in the lead car, behind the State Highway Patrol escort, in the triumphant parade overland across ancient Carlos Bay for the first time in history. Also, during the free-from-toll period of two hours that followed the ribbon-cutting ceremony, 1,120 automobiles crossed to the islands carrying the greatest number of people that had crossed to the islands in one day (except during the seashell show) in the past thousands of years.

After the bridge opening, the little mail boat *Santiva* still ran but only for a few more months until its mail contract expired. The Singletons had operated it from 1936 until 1952 when the Palmer Ladds (Palmer, his wife, Myrtle, and brother-in-law, Brewton Walters) had taken over. By that time, the mail boat trip had become a delightful scenic excursion for tourists in addition to delivering mail, island passengers, and freight.

The *Santiva* continued to shop for a few islanders who never cared to go upriver to town. Captain Ladd purchased hardware, ice, crates of milk in glass bottles and the like while Myrtle handled the more delicate items like clothing, cosmetics, linens, and bras. The Ladds' day began at 6:00 a.m. Mail and freight had to be picked up at the Fort Myers

231

Post Office and train. These and other cargoes were stowed aboard as they were delivered to the boat.

About 8:00 a.m., the tourists began arriving at the dock. They wore slacks or shorts, carried sunglasses, wore big hats, carried lunch. There was a glass enclosed cabin but travelers usually clambered topside and seated themselves merrily upon the gaily painted red, white, and blue benches that would accommodate thirty-five people.

Downriver, past Thomas A. Edison's winter home and on toward the wild freedom of the lower Caloosa Hatchee, the sturdy mail boat sailed toward the islands. Then Captain Ladd would turn his wheel over to Brewton Walters and climb topside to talk with the tourists up there in the salt-tanged air under the sun.

He would point out for them the birds nesting in mangrove jungles on small islands they were passing, and shell mounds where the ancients had lived.

There were playful porpoises and curious needlefish following the boat and sometimes silver kings rolled in fishy splendor through the waters.

Atop Channel Marker No. 7 there was an eagle's nest and an osprey's nest atop another.

Passing Punta Rassa, Ladd pointed out the old Summerlin (Towle's) House built on heavy pilings, defying sea and wind as it had since old cattle days when bellowing herds of long-horns had been shipped from there over docks that were no more.

When the mail boat reached Sanibel dock, some of the passengers would get off and walk over to the Gulf to gather seashells. Others would ride on to Saint James City and Captiva.

On a close-in sandbar near Captiva there might be raccoons and pink spoonbills feeding. Along the way crates of lettuce, cabbages, boxes of bread, cakes of ice, sewing thread or a special bra were put off at landings where someone waited, as was mail at certain points, and occasionally an islander returning home.

The opening of the Sanibel Bridge had meant the end of all this was at hand.

Artist's sketch of mail boat's last run (*Santiva*).—By Eleanor Douglas Clapp

December 9, 1963, the *Santiva* made her last run. There were sixteen passengers aboard for the journey. When Sanibel landing was reached a small crowd of island dwellers awaited this final arrival and nineteen more passengers came aboard for the last ride.

With three sentimental boats following, the *Santiva* headed for old Saint James and then for Captiva.

At Captiva more than fifty mail-boat fans were gathered at the dock to say "farewell." Postmistress, Mrs. Ray Booth, and Dale Ballinger strewed flowers on the waters and islanders and passengers sang: "Auld Lang Syne."

As the *Santiva* left Captiva landing for the last time, sirens blew and seven boats fell in line to escort her on her lonely journey back to Sanibel and upriver.

No more would water travelers smile at the note from Pauline Bailey to her too busy husband of yesterday, pinned on the wall of old Bailey's store on Sanibel:

> I'm waiting on the briny deep
> One date with you I'd love to keep
> My sole requirement for a rendezvous
> Is just one motor, boat, and YOU.

233

Nor would passengers grin when they visited Captiva's tiny post office fronting the Bay and landing with Stars and Stripes floating in the breeze, and then read on the wall of Timmie's Nook nearby:

> The difficult age has come and lit
> Too tired to work . . . too poor to quit. . . .

Henceforth, mail or lumber, cokes or goats, they would be delivered over landfill and bridges from the mainland by truck.

Mail had come to the islands via railroad steamer, the Kinzie steamers, the Singleton mail boat and Ladd's mail boat. Now the mail boat would be no more. And the ferries were already gone.

With them went the seaborne way of life that islanders had known for more than three-quarters of a century—that the old islands had known for thousands of years. For good or ill (and only time would know the truth) the islands were attached to the mainland and hordes of the curious would come across Carlos Bay at will.

On the day that the bridge was opened a mainland real estate man had remarked: *"The isolation of Sanibel Island is ended and we must not allow the full significance of this day to escape us as we watch the removal of a barrier which has kept intact this gift of our generation—."*

The Fort Myers *Press* that day editorialized: "The picturesque resort islands of Sanibel and Captiva enter a new era today . . . and the impact will be heavy on the mainland as well. The isolation of the two islands—of their shelling beaches and other attractions, of their resort facilities and of their residents—is ended and they become integrated into the body of Lee County. . . .

"For all the islanders . . . the bridge brings convenience, and many amenities and to most it will bring economic gain. . . .

"For some who prized . . . isolation, the bridge that wipes it away is unwelcome. Scores of persons from all over the country who had visited Sanibel, along with some island residents, signed petitions and wrote letters protesting the plans

234

Such tiny landings as the above, left Sanibel, right Captiva, would henceforth see the mail boat no more. On Sanibel the mail was put off at the landing and a "dispatcher" carried it around the shore of the Bay to the little post office on the road to the ferry landing for sorting and delivering. On Captiva mail was put off at a separate landing from Andy's although the *Santiva* "guests" nearly always visited Andy's for the atmosphere of the sea.—*Hello Stranger* collection

to build the bridge. One group fought it in the courts. They apprehended that the tranquility they found at Sanibel and Captiva and the unspoiled natural attractions of the islands would be destroyed. Time alone can tell whether these apprehensions were well grounded. . . ."

As assets for the bridge, the paper suggested: "It will mean a good deal . . . to be able to get to Fort Myers or elsewhere at any hour of the day or night . . . Island school children can participate in extra-curricular activities from which the transportation situation previously barred them; persons stricken ill or incurring accidents can have prompt access to hospital and medical attention; businessmen and housewives will find their errands on the mainland greatly facilitated; travelers, whether island residents or tourists, no longer need adjust their schedule to that of the ferries. . . ."

To all these, islanders rebelled. They recalled that nobody had wanted to go anywhere much and if they did the ferries were good enough. There were only a few children who needed "extra-curricular school activities."

In all history, people had seldom been inconvenienced when ill or dying: in the past they would have died anyway, in recent time there had been the seaplane offering excellent ambulance service.

The mail boat had met needs of shopping for housewives of the islands and travelers who did not want to adjust their schedules to that of the ferries did not really have to come to the islands at all.

Economic gain—the bane of modern civilization—had never bothered islanders too much. They had lived from day to day. They had enjoyed their friends, their seclusion, the absence of heavy traffic and odors; their time to gather seashells, to write, paint pictures, observe wildlife, or do nothing.

Nevertheless, the $2,805,081 bridge—a magnificent achievement of engineering beauty—was out there across the bay, hooking the islands to the mainland, perhaps forever. It was defiantly built out where great Gulf storms would beat upon it. It would block, to a great extent, present and future use of the old harbor of Carlos (San Carlos Bay).

But where once galleons and pirogues fought bitterly to keep Conquistadores from subjugating them and changing their island world, travelers would speed over and through the waters, via bridge and causeway, and inevitably changes would follow. . . .

Epilogue

Tomorrow is here . . .

The new Sanibel Causeway is open twenty-four hours a day. Toll is paid at the Punta Rassa tollbooth where you leave the mainland. An automobile, including all passengers, pays three dollars to cross old Carlos Bay. Motorcycles and motor bikes pay four dollars. There is no charge for the return trip.

Leaving the tollbooth your smooth pathway takes you through pastel-colored waters. Fishermen are cast fishing from the shores. Offshore, men are fishing from boats. Along the sands at one point there are signs that say: "Bird Crossing! Caution!" They are to protect sea terns which nest there at certain seasons of the year.

Approaching Sanibel Island, on your left, is the Light House and Point Ybel. To your right lies Woodring Point, and along the bay shore, toward that point is where so many of the earliest homesteaders built their homes and docks where steamers came with mail, merchandise and visitors.

As you drive off the causeway, it is only a short distance to Periwinkle Drive (S 867). There you may turn left toward the Light House or right and drive the length of Sanibel and over Ciego or Blind Pass to Captiva.

Both islands now have numerous motels, hotels, and inns along the Gulf shore, around the Bay, along the roadway, most of them half hidden away. Each island has a post office, a volunteer fire department, and a small public library. One integrated grade school serves both islands. There are five modest churches and scattered about are excellent restaurants, shops that sell seashells and art supplies, gas stations

237

Mrs. Flora Woodring Morris, first white child born on Sanibel Island, displaying pieces of pottery on the lower shelves of her whatnot. This is a part of the collection she gathered in her early girlhood days on Sanibel.—Photo Mrs. John Morris

and beauty salons. There is an amazingly cosmopolitan bookshop, and a unique seasonal theatre—and even (on Sanibel) a small shopping center.

Down Bailey's Road, the Sanibel Packing Company that served the islands once with needles and kerosene, rubber boots and harness, had outgrown itself, expanded, and a second store built. It washed away in a storm and a third place was erected in a palm grove on a shell elevation. Now the store called "Bailey's" is located in the shopping center where Periwinkle Drive meets Tarpon Bay Road, and is operated by Francis Bailey, descendant of the original Bailey brothers.

The store they left behind on the Bay is called "The Red Pelican" and sells: "Gifts from 35 countries, Mexican imports, *penny candy* and *salmagundi.*"

The ancient shell ridges and mounds have been dug into, leveled, or gradually transported via barge upriver to make beds for highways—yet memories still blaze around the Bay.

The sounds of bulldozers and draglines may trouble you as you drive the winding roads among coconut palms to "Lost Colony," but red hibiscus flowers will lure you on, and sweet perfume of oleanders hold promise of lazy days in the sun.

238

On the Gulf front, Casa Ybel and Island Inn have modernized with the times. Gray Gables is still reminiscent of the days when its downstairs was a dining room and kitchen; there are still Confederate flags and intricate genealogical charts upstairs; and out front, beyond the neatly kept old home, roll the translucent waters framed by pines and palms through which the ancient trade winds still blow.

Along the old road to Wulfert thick casuarina trees make dark shadows where pink and white oleanders bloom. These were planted by the Chadwicks of Captiva along with their "plantations" of coconut palms and Honduras limes. One of Frank Henderson's girls, Mrs. Annie Allred, and others of her kin, have returned to Wulfert to live out their days in neat new homes by old Dinkins Bayou, surrounded by low rosebushes and scarlet bougainvillea.

Stella Mitchell, now in her nineties, lives by the waters of Blind Pass still. On the bank are empty chairs under coconut palms but the old home is freshly painted and stands in plain view of the new concrete bridge that replaced the picturesque but too old wooden one in 1954.

The still living islanders of yesterday are sentimental folk. Take Clarence Rutland, who has a nursery of coconut palms and raises tropical flowers. Each day he picks fresh hibiscus blooms and lays them on the living room table—because his deceased wife, Ruth, always kept flowers there.

And there is Scotia Bryant who lives a short way from the Light House. She picks garden flowers when they are available (and wild galardias, called Sanibel daisies, when they are not) and tucks them in a china vase in remembrance of her mother. The vase came with the family to their homestead on Captiva in the far away past.

Equally sentimental in their way are the new old-timers who came to the islands in the 1940's and 1950's. Consider the quaint Captive Post Office: Inside there are usually beautiful golden-yellow hibiscus flowers and frosted pink ones that Jean Hayford brings each day from her garden. Outside the post office in winter there are often exhibits of local artists with sometimes nostalgic scenes from their New Eng-

239

Left: Coconut palms and casuarina trees along sand-shell road to the Light House today.

Right: Aged, twisted buttonwood tree and big rain tank by one of the Light House dwellings today.—*Hello Stranger* collection

Sanibel Light is still needed for navigation, because the islands still protrude into the path of northbound ships sailing the coast. It is still a landfall light, marking the entrance to San Carlos Bay, the Caloosa Hatchee and Charlotte Harbor from the south.

The Coast Guard has been removed. The 13,000 candlepower Light is "unwatched," electrically operated with power stubbed from the mainland. It has storage batteries that take over automatically in event of power failure. There are four extra bulbs, each coming on automatically as others burn out. The rays of the sun turn the light out in the morning, darkness brings light on again at night.—L. L. Cook photo

240

But trade winds still blow across Point Ybel and picturesque shrimp trawlers now sail by in pairs, out into the Gulf and head for Tortugas or the Campeche banks of Mexico.—*Hello Stranger* collection

land or Middle Western homes along with those of the islands.

Andy's on Captiva has changed little. He presides over Andy's primitive dock where beer and coffee are drunk and tall tales are spun. You may still hear of the Sanibel alcoholic, son of an ambassador, artist of a sort, who periodically went on sprees and afterward always painted his body green to show remorse. Assuredly, you may hear of the auto wreck that happened when there were only two cars on Captiva.

In the best Southern plantation style, the now luxurious South Seas Plantation has added tall white pillars to one of its buildings, and laid out—in view of rolling Gulf and murmuring Sound—a modern golf course where palms lean grotesquely in the trade winds and flowers are perpetually in bloom.

Other changes have come to the islands. Instead of the palm-thatched dwellings of aborigines and homesteaders, there is now a variety of homes, large and small, some built at ground level, others ten feet off the sands. The most unusual have been built since 1950.

The William E. Stevensons' home (housing their seashell collection and Southeast Asian souvenirs) is said to be of "Filipino style"; that of the Joseph Van Flecks of "Japanese simplicity."

Colonel and Mrs. Aycock, who lived in Manila and Tokyo six years, have an "oriental style" home, which is reached

241

through rich plantings of bamboo, papyrus, and Japanese honeysuckle. There is a small red pagoda on a rock near the "stunning brass-trimmed door," and there are Far Eastern furnishings and *objects d'art* within.

Hidden away among lovely old trees and tropical shrubbery is the home of the Walter W. Watts (he is vice-president of R.C.A.), which is said to suggest an Italian villa.

On a windswept point is the C. F. Siegenthaler place with its tinge of Polynesian appearance. Through large glass doors and picture windows there are glimpses of the open rolling sea.

The Ernest Stantons' home has the special attraction of a screened patio with its ceiling open to the sky, and through windows of the living room, a view of the majestic Gulf.

Probably the most astonishing of island homes is the Mississippi River steamboat *Algiers,* converted by the Lathrop Browns into a dwelling place with six master bedrooms and five and a half baths, some of which had French marble

Drive slowly and breathe deeply of salt air as you ride along Periwinkle Drive on Sanibel. There tall trees rise upward and vegetation creeps to the very edge of the trails—and sun and shadows will take you back in time.

Peer into the vegetation along the way. Although it is well over a century since the first sisal plants were set out on Sanibel, you may see descendants growing wild.

In isolated locations you will occasionally see a castor bean plant, relative of those planted in the 1860's that were used to make castor oil to treat Confederate prisoners of war on Tortugas Island after the War Between the States.—*Hello Stranger* collection

lavatories and gold fixtures—and there was a passenger elevator connecting the three decks, or floors.

The *Algiers* became quite a lady. She had been towed around the Gulf of Mexico from New Orleans and upriver to Fort Myers. There she was renovated, then towed to Sanibel's Gulf shore. A channel was cut across the sandy beach and a quarter of a mile inland to a pond. This channel was just deep and wide enough for the steamboat which was thereafter carefully "worked" along inland through it. At the same time, bulldozers followed behind, filling in the channel again.

When the steamboat reached the pond, a steel hull and steel caissons steadied her and workmen began pouring tons of crushed seashells and sand underneath and around her.

At last the *Algiers* sat in matronly aloofness on dry land with her twin smokestacks lifted against the sky and her paddle wheel still attached to her stern.

She was surrounded by twenty-five acres of land and 990 feet of Gulf beach and sparkling waters for her front garden—she was valued at half a million dollars in the 1960's.

You may not see these homes for they are on the Gulf shore and reached by winding secretive roadways; but they are there, and quite a contrast to the palm-thatched dwellings of the aborigines and homesteaders of days now gone.

You may, however, visit the home areas of the wild birds for the islands are still a take-off point for migratory flights of seabirds heading for South America. There are still vast mangrove areas for rookeries where birds may roost for a night or nest for a season. There are sloughs, fresh water, minute sea creatures in saltwater shallows and brackish bayous, and on land wild sea oats, sea grapes, and a variety of seed grasses for food.

The best place to visit the birds is in the J. N. "Ding" Darling Wildlife Sanctuary on Sanibel. A one-way road winds through it and a canoe trail is mapped for visitors. Alligators and otter live in the sloughs and marshes. From an observation tower there you may sometimes witness spectacular shows, especially in the morning and evening when birds go out or return from feeding on surrounding sandbars and mud flats of Bay and Sound.

243

Some time before you reach the shopping center and Coconut Grove Restaurant, you'll pass Harbor House, which was once Jack's Place where the "Old Goat" and Gert held forth. It's all changed now but outside is the air raid shelter he built in the 1950's so that he and Gert could "ride out an atomic bomb attack and emerge later to start a brave new world." His Sanibel tomato patch is gone, but the bananas still bear purple blooms and sometimes a stalk of bananas hangs there in the sun.—*Hello Stranger* collection

Cries for establishment of this sanctuary came in 1962 as the new bridge was being constructed. The sudden changes and growth of the islands caused old-timers and new old-timers and even visitors to become fearful for the ecology of the region.

Away back in 1949 the F. P. Bailey Wildlife Refuge of eighty acres of marsh and slough off Tarpon Bay Road had been established. This, apparently, the wild birds knew. Within five years 22,000 ducks came in fall; roseate spoonbills, down to 38 in 1940 increased to 175.

Before this, in 1945, the Sanibel Island Wildlife Refuge had been established. Presumably it embraced 12,000 acres. Actually it was mostly individually owned homes, hotels, motels, and businesses. Only a small part was owned by the state or government, and wildlife was protected mainly through enthusiastic cooperation of the islanders. Moreover, the Bailey Refuge was only *leased* to the Fish and Wildlife Service.

With the coming of the bridge and land speculators, there was need for permanent plans if any wildlife was to be pre-

The old Sanibel schoolhouse (see page 113). Hurricane Donna of 1960 blew off the belfry and the bell disappeared, but who cared? A new integrated school was built elsewhere and Philip and Ruth Hunter (she famous for seven years acting in *Tobacco Road*) used the old one for a Pirate's Theatre.

Pirate Theatre operates only in winter, accommodates eighty-eight spectators but averages ninety to a hundred somehow. Islanders ride by and call: "Save me seven" or "I want eight," meaning they want seats reserved for a show.—*Hello Stranger* collection

served for wildlife was the background and heart of island living. So islanders joined with state and government and thousands of acres of natural wilderness were set aside and dedicated to wildlife forever. It was named after Darling because he had championed wildlife everywhere for more than fifty years.

It will take time and patience to visit the birds. Yet, whether you ride quietly through the sanctuary by car, or paddle a canoe through the waterway, or walk leisurely along, or sit up in the observation tower with binoculars—you will be transported back into the ages as the wild birds go about their old ways of life in the twentieth century.

About the season when the birds fly south, great schools of certain fish make their fall migrations down the Gulf to warmer waters also. At such times the aborigines came to catch fish and salt or smoke them. Now sportsmen come from everywhere to join the exciting thrills of capturing fighting fish—for food and trophies.

Simultaneous with the coming of the *pajares de paso* and the *pescados de paso,* tourist homes are opened for human visitors and hotels for seasonal visitors. There will be gay people, wearing bright red, yellow, or rainbow-colored swim-

245

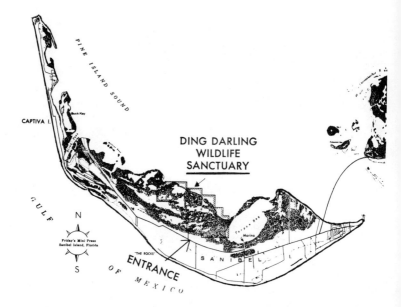

Map of the J. N. (Ding) Darling Wildlife Sanctuary (not to be confused with the Bailey Wildlife Refuge) was established by the U.S. Government after Darling's death in 1962.

The sanctuary is under management of the Fish and Wildlife Service, Department of the Interior, with local headquarters in one of the Light House dwellings of old Point Ybel. Bird lists and information can be obtained there.

ming suits, some of them relaxing under coconut palms or beach umbrellas on the white sandy shores near the sea-green waters.

Soon, the islands will be aglow and atwitter with Christmas trees, Christmas festivities, quaint services in the small churches, and dancing elsewhere.

During the winter, by the Hartman's home on Gulf Drive which has been occupied in season by different generations for more than half a century, you may see an interesting sight. There will be old orange and grapefruit trees laden with golden and yellow fruit, a Japanese orchid tree, perhaps in bloom, and sometimes a few Sanibel tomatoes still growing among other vegetables in "kitchen" gardens.

Spring comes very early to these waters. Native fish, mollusks and crustaceans give birth to billions of young in the

Lost in the wonder of the sea. Above is a modern small boy with a giant-size *fascialora gigantica,* wondering—as men through the ages—at the miracles of the sea.

Island children play sailing ships, observe nests of seabirds along the shore, duck their heads when ungainly pelicans sail overhead in the twilight and flap their big wings on their way to rookeries of surrounding islands.—Florida State News Bureau photo

shallows and deeps in January and February. Many of them will furnish food for the wild birds as they return in February and March on their spring migratory flights north as well as for the schools of fish that went south who will return in flashing glory, and the mighty silver kings that will roll again in the deep passes and bays.

You may join seashell lovers and conchologists from over the world by visiting the Sanibel-Captiva Shell Show in March; peer into the glass tanks of seawater where deep-sea specimens lurk; wander along thatched shelters out in the open to look upon paintings of local scenes by island artists.

In summer, before rains come, the rainfrogs will croak persistent warnings. Soon, without fail, the rain will come. Liquid veils of silver sometimes shot through with sun will drench the islands and cool the semi-tropic world. Afterward sometimes white gulls will be seen flying in the gray skies of the departing storm while a rainbow suddenly arches in color-ful beauty above the roiling sea.

All year, you will learn, the tides come higher and recede lower at the time of the new and full moon. Then young and old go forth to wade the exposed shallows and sand bars and explore "tide pools" that are usually hidden from human sight; and observe seashells and sea creatures that seem amaz-ingly like humankind when you enter their secret worlds.

You, like many strangers to the islands, may be filled with wonder at the ebb tide hour when the sea has withdrawn itself from the land and there is a still, waiting period, a breathless hush offshore. Then, as the tide begins to turn, will come the faint far away sounds of the "turn of the tide," and small incoming waves will begin to clutch at the shore and grow in strength until at long last there is the flood tide once more.

So it was when the homesteaders inhabited the islands, and the Spaniards came, and the Caloosas lived far back in time—part of the cycles of the seas of the world, of the Universal Pattern of the Unseen and Unknown.

If you are up at dawn, the waters may be milky blue or milky rose in lovely color—and still as glass. Gradually light suffuses the surroundings, a small breeze stirs the waters,

Not snow but white sugar-sand of old Tarpon Bay Road to the Gulf. It's paved now. There's parking space at the end but cars are barred from travel to the shore. Still, there are wild sea grapes, Australian pines, cacti . . . the sound and sight of the lovely Gulf of Mexico . . .—*Hello Stranger* collection

birds, and the sea awakens, and island dwellers begin their day.

In the sunset a flight of wood ibis, or white egrets, or pink curlews will glide across the colorful sky, making startling contrast with the still green of the mangrove jungles and blue seas around the Bay—while human life will go its way in the homes and hotels on the islands below.

In the moonlight, across the big orange-yellow disk of the island moon, a dark cloud moves. There is darkness, then light again as the cloud passes and a bright pathway will suddenly lie across the dark waters while the moonlight will make dark silhouettes of the exotic coconut palms on the shore.

At nine o'clock, if it be summer, in old island gardens, the night-blooming *cereus,* "Queen of the Night," will open gorgeous huge blossoms of white that will perfume the air with seductive fragrance.

On the "dark of the moon" you may sometimes see shadowy figures here and there, with flashlights, walking along the tide lines of the sugar-sands. They will be seashell collectors, hoping to snatch some special seashell that may be cast up by the rising or lowering tide.

And all the while—for those who know—there will be the still faint echoes of the past: of ancient ones and temple fires across the Bay . . . of sails of galleons and armored Spaniards . . . of homesteaders, early settlers and coastal traders . . . of steamboat bells and whistles . . . the sounds of laughter and stomp of square dancers at the Light House . . . and the sounds of a master's violin. . . .

You will no longer wonder, as you ride these roadways or walk the sands of these islands, "Who came here? Who went away? What happened long ago?"

But you may again speak to the shuffling old man trudging along like a phantom in the dusk (Is he Indian? Is he Spaniard?—You still may not know): "What will happen to these islands now that the outside world is moving in over the causeways and bridges, and the bulldozers and draglines have come?"

With a gentle shrug, he may once more answer you as he passes on: "*¿Quién sabe, señor* (or *señora* or *señorita* as the case may be)? *Quién sabe?*"

Who knows? Who knows?

White road of shell and sand along the shore where horses and carriages and "Granny" Matthews' ponies traveled leisurely long ago. Left, are shimmering translucent green waters and white foam on silver sands. Right is dense tropical shrubbery.—*Hello Stranger* collection

APPENDIX

Notes

Primary sources for information regarding the history of Sanibel and Captiva are included in the Acknowledgments in the front of this book. Other sources are cited briefly here by chapters and full information will be found in the Bibliography which follows.

Chapter 1
Island prelude to human history . . .
1. George R. Cooley, *The Vegetation of Sanibel Island, Lee County, Florida,* pp. 269-89.
2. John H. Davis, Jr., Ph.D., *The Natural Features of Southern Florida,* p. 63.
3. Charles Ledyard Norton, *A Handbook of Florida,* pp. 260-61.
4. Cooley, p. 272.

Chapter 2
Shell mounds and pile dwellings . . .
1. Francis P. Fleming, *Memoirs of Florida,* p. 378.
2. Frank H. Cushing, *Exploration of Ancient Key-dweller Remains of the Gulf Coast of Florida,* p. 345.
3. Florence Fritz, *Unknown Florida,* p. 22.
4. Cushing, p. 345.
5. Ibid., pp. 345-46.
6. Although Cushing called it "Ellis Bay," this was Tarpon Bay. It was customary then to name bays and bayous for inhabitants who lived close by.
7. Cushing, pp. 346-47.
8. *The Florida Anthropologist,* Vol. 2, Nos. 3-4, November 1941, p. 74. "Incised pottery artifacts, Sanibel Island. A type of the Glades series, decorated with designs formed by rows of small tick marks (Goddin, 1944; Willey, 1949a, Pl. 3, K). These usually form simple chevron or running V designs."
9. Many of the shell mounds have been destroyed by shell dealers and others. The material of them makes fine base for paths, trails, and roadways.

Chapter 3
Ybel y Cautivo, and Pedro Menendez . . .

1. T. Frederick Davis, *History of Juan Ponce de Leon's Voyages to Florida*, article.

2. Fritz, pp. 25-26; Barcia, p. 6.

3. Andres G. Barcia, *Caballido y Zuniga, Ensayo cronologico para la Historia general de la Florida*, p. 6.

4. *Oviedo*, Vol. 3, p. 622. Shea, *The Catholic Church in Colonial Days*, p. 102.

5. John R. Swanton, *Final Report of the U.S. DeSoto Expedition Commission*.

6. Fritz, p. 39.

Chapter 4
Missionaries, pescadores, and pirates . . .

1. Barcia.

2. Bernard Romans, Esq., *A Concise Natural History of East and West Florida*.

3. Ibid., pp. 126-27.

4. Ibid., pp. 1, 193.

5. Ibid., p. 1.

6. Ibid., pp. 193, 279.

7. David O. True, *Pirates and Treasure Trove of South Florida*, article.

Chapter 5
Sanybel, sugarcane and soldiers . . .

1. James W. Covington, Ph.D., *The Story of Southwestern Florida*, p. 741.

2. John Lee Williams, *The Territory of Florida, . . . etc.*, p. 32.

3. Ibid., pp. 287, 288, 291.

4. Ibid., pp. 33, 294.

5. Ibid., p. 33.

6. Ibid., p. 27.

7. John T. Sprague, *The Origin, Progress, and Conclusion of the Florida War*, pp. 228-29.

8. Ibid., 233.

9. Ibid., p. 235.

10. Ibid., pp. 233, 234, 235, 236.

Chapter 6
Sisal, another war, and castor beans . . .

1. *U.S. Department of Agriculture yearbook*, 1856, article.

2. Fritz, *Unknown Florida*, pp. 69-73.

3. Civil War Naval Chronology 1861-1865, Part V-1865, *Attack on Fort Myers*, pp. 53, 54, 58. Photostats in author's file.

4. *East Gulf Blockading Squadron,* Official Records of the Union and Confederate Navies in the War of the Rebellion. Photostats of pages 812, 814, 823, in author's file.

5. Official Records Service, History Division, Navy Department, vol. I, p. 103. Photostat in author's file.

6. Fritz, p. 79.

7. Ibid., p. 75.

Chapter 7
The Light House and Point Ybel . . .

1. Correspondence with U.S. Archives and Light House Site file of Florida, Bundle No. 44, Reports and Records of the Light House Board, 1877 to July 8, 1888. File includes U.S. Treasury reports, Department of Commerce Light House service and numerous electro-stat copies of correspondence, orders, deeds, blueprints, etc., in author's file. Hereinafter referred to as L.H. Board or L.H. Board records.

2. Ibid., letters December 31, 1877, to July 8, 1888.

3. Ibid., undated, unidentified memorandum concerning status of title to lands on Sanibel.

4. Ibid., L.H. Board reports August 15, 1883, showing relinquishment of title to Sanibel by Governor W. D. Bloxham for state of Florida to the U.S. Also, abstract of L.H. contracts Vol. 1, p. 69, showing contract was executed August 29, 1883, for metal work on the Sanibel light.

5. Ibid., L.H.B. report, 1884.

6. Ibid., L.H.B. report August 20, 1885.

7. Report of Collector of Customs, Key West, Fla., in L.H.B. file of 1884.

Chapter 8
Woodring Point and Tarpon Bay . . .

1. U.S. Census of 1870 on microfilm from U.S. Department of Archives, at Key West Public Library, courtesy of the Key West Historical Society.

2. Ibid.

3. Romans, p. 128.

Chapter 9
Early settlers on Gulf front and Bay . . .

1. The material in this chapter was gathered mainly from interviews with early settlers themselves, supplemented by clippings in files of the author.

Chapter 10
Pine Island Sound and Carlos Bay . . .

1. Steamboating information obtained from interviews with Effie Winkler Henderson McAdow, who rode steamboats when a girl on these

waters; from Arthur Gibson, who as boy and youth worked on the steamers; and others in addition to clippings in the author's file.

2. L.H.B. records of 1890.

3. Ibid., 1890.

4. Ibid., 1891 and 1892.

5. Clippings from old *Press* files, 1892, in author's file.

6. Ibid., July 12, 1892.

7. L.H.B. records of March 28, 1896.

8. Ibid.

9. Lee County Courthouse, Fort Myers, Florida, Miscellaneous Records, Book 1, p. 215.

10. Correspondence with U.S. Post Office Department, Deputy Special Assistant to the Postmaster General D. Jamison Cain, July 22, 1968.

11. Ibid.

12. Photostat copy of *History of the Rural Free Delivery Service*, in author's file with correspondence of July 22, 1968.

Chapter 11
Sanibel tomatoes, Wulfert, and mosquitoes . . .

1. Eleanor G. Pearse, *Florida's Vanishing Era.*

2. Records U.S.P.O., Fort Myers, Florida, courtesy Ellis Solomon, postmaster.

3. Interview with Mrs. Annie Allred, April 1968.

4. Interview with Mrs. Pearl Stokes, May 1968.

Chapter 12
Captiva area's ups and downs . . .

1. Material in this chapter was gathered from old-timers themselves and their descendants.

Chapter 13
Light House problems, war, and St. Patrick's Day . . .

1. L.H.B. records, résumé of events that had taken place on the L.H. Reservation at Sanibel, from the Department of Commerce, Light House Service, Key West, Florida, dated April 10, 1925.

2. L.H.B. records of December 14, 1882.

3. Ibid., April 10, 1925.

4. Ibid., Special Report, 1896.

5. Fritz, *Unknown Florida*, p. 103.

6. Ibid.

7. From Letitia Nutt's scrapbooks, still extant, in Gray Gables, on Sanibel.

Chapter 14
Book learnin' by the sea . . .

1. *History of the Lee County Schools*, unpublished manuscript by E. H. "Ned" Loveland, on file in Southwest Florida Historical Society files and in Lee County Schools office.

(Note: Deviations and additions to the island section of the above manuscript are caused by the author's personal knowledge or from interviews with old-timers who actually attended the schools on the islands.)

2. Ibid.

3. Ibid.

4. Interview with Clarence Rutland who remembers both buildings well as they were in the vicinity of his home.

5. Letitia Nutt scrapbook.

6. Jesse Carter, now in his eighties, remembers this well.

7. Ibid.

Chapter 15 through 25 and Epilogue . . .

Material for the balance of these chapters is contained in interviews and clippings in files of the author.

Bibliography

Andrews, Charles M. "The Florida Indians in the Seventeenth Century." *Tequesta*, Vol. 1, No. 3. Coral Gables, July 1943.

Barcia, Andres G. *Caballido y Zuniga, Ensayo cronologico para la Historia general de la Florida.* Madrid, 1723.

Conner, Jeanette Thurber. *Pedro Menendez de Aviles Memorial*, by Gonzalo Salis DeMeras. Deland, 1923.

Cooke, C. Wythe. "Scenery of Florida, Interpreted by a Geologist." Florida Department of Conservation, *Geological Bulletin* No. 17. Tallahassee, 1939.

Cooley, George R. "The Vegetation of Sanibel Island, Lee County, Florida." *Rhodora*, Vol. 57, No. 682 (October 1955), (Journal of the New England Botanical Club, 8-10 West King Street, Lancaster, Pennsylvania; Botanical Museum, Oxford Street, Cambridge, Mass.).

Covington, James W., Ph.D. *The Story of Southwestern Florida*, Vol. 1. New York: Lewis Historical Publishing Company, 1957.

Cushing, Frank H. "Exploration of Ancient Key-dweller Remains of the Gulf Coast of Florida." *Proceedings of the American Philosophical Society*, Vol. 35. Philadelphia, December 1896.

Davis, John H., Jr., Ph.D. "The Natural Features of Southern Florida." *Geological Bulletin No. 25*, Florida Geological Survey. Tallahassee, Fla., 1943.

Davis, T. Frederick. "History of Ponce de Leon's Voyages to Florida." *Florida Historical Quarterly*, Vol. 14 (July 1935).

Dimock, A. W. *Florida Enchantments.* New York, 1915.

Dimock, A. W. *The Book of the Tarpon.* New York, 1915.

Dodd, Dorothy. "The Wrecking Business on the Florida Reef, 1822-1860." *Florida Historical Quarterly*, No. 4. Gainesville, 1934.

Fairbanks, George R. *The Story of Florida.* Philadelphia: J. E. Lippincott and Company, 1871.

Fewkes, J. W. "Aboriginal Wooden Objects from Southern Florida," Smithsonian Institution, *Miscellaneous Collections*, Vol. 80, No. 9 (1928).

Fleming, Francis P. *Memoirs of Florida.* Atlanta, Ga.: The Southern Historical Association, 1902.

Fritz, Florence. *Unknown Florida*, Coral Gables: University of Miami Press, 1963.

261

Gatewood, George W. *Ox-Cart Days to Airplane Era in Southern Florida.* Punta Gorda, Fla.: Punta Gorda Herald Press, 1939.

Gatewood, George W. *Coconut Coasts.* Punta Gorda, Fla.: Punta Gorda Herald Press, 1939.

Green, Edwin L., Ph.D. *School History of Florida.* Baltimore, 1899.

Harrington, M. R. "Cuba Before Columbus, Indian Notes and Monographs." *Miscellaneous,* Museum of the American Indian, No. 17, New York, 1921.

McNicoll, Robert E. "The Caloosa Village Tequesta." *Tequesta Magazine,* Vol. 1, No. 1. Coral Gables: March 1941.

Norton, Charles Ledyard. *A Handbook of Florida, with 49 Maps and Plans.* Third Edition, Revised (New York 1892).

Pearse, Eleanor D. *Florida's Vanishing Era.* Privately published, 1954.

Peters, Thelma. "Blockade-Running in the Bahamas During the Civil War." *Tequesta,* No. 5. Coral Gables, 1945.

Romans, Bernard, Esq. *A Concise Natural History of East and West Florida.* Originally published in New York. Facsimile reprint, with introduction by Louise Richardson, A.B. and M.A. New Orleans: Pelican Publishing Company, 1961.

Schellings, Wm. J., Ed. "On-Blockade Duty in Florida Waters." *Tequesta XV,* Coral Gables.

Sprague, John T., Brevt. Capt. 8th Reg. U.S. Infantry. *The Origin, Progress and Conclusion of the Florida War.* New York: D. Appleton and Company, 1848.

Swanton, John. "The Indians of the Southeastern U.S." Bureau of American Ethnology, *Bulletin 137.* Washington, 1946.

Swanton, John R. *Final Report of the U.S.-DeSoto Expedition.* Washington, D.C.: U.S. Government Printing Office, 1939.

Tebeau, Charlton W. *Florida's Last Frontier.* Coral Gables: University of Miami Press, 1957.

"Tekesta Indians of Southern Florida." *Florida Historical Quarterly,* Vol. 28. Gainesville, 1940.

True, David O. *Imago Mvndi, A Review of Early Cartography.* Edited by Leo Bagrow, Anno DNI MCMLIV, Stockholm. Compilation of best maps of the Conquistadores.

True, David O. "Pirates and Treasure Trove of South Florida." *Tequesta.* Coral Gables, 1946.

Varner, John Grier, and Varner, Jeanette Johnson. "The Florida of the Inca." *Garcilasco de la Vaga.* Austin, Texas, 1951.

Willey, Gordon R. "Archaeology of the Florida Gulf Coast." Smithsonian *Miscellaneous Collections,* Vol. 113. Washington, 1949.

Williams, John Lee. *The Territory of Florida: or Sketches Topography, Civil and Natural History of the Country, the Climate, and the Indian Tribes from the First Discovery to the Present Time.* With an introduction by Herbert J. Doherty, Jr. Facsimile reproduction of the 1837 edition. Gainesville: University of Florida Press, 1962.

262

Newspapers and Guides

Fort Myers *Weekly Press* and Fort Myers *News Press,* 1884-1968.
Hello Stranger! Magazine and guides, Fort Myers, Fla., 1944-1961.
Tropical News, Fort Myers, Fla., 1895-1929.

Maps

1500-1700	David O. True, *Imago Mvndi* (see above).
1823	John Lee Williams, *Map of Florida.*
1840	*Map of East Florida,* Capt. John Mackay and Lieut. J. E. Blake. Published by order of the U.S. Senate.
1856	*Military Map of the Peninsula of Florida, South of Tampa Bay,* published by order to Hon. Jefferson Davis, secretary of war, U.S. War Department.
1891	Maps of waterways, steamship routes and railroads of Florida, Norton's Guide 1892.
1948	Map: *Gulf Coast of Florida, Estero Bay to Lemon Bay, Including Charlotte Harbor.* U.S. Coast and Geodetic Survey, 5th Edition. Washington, D.C., 1948.
	Also maps of roads, state of Florida, 1925; and other state road department, etc., maps, dated 1900-1968.

Index

Names of Island inhabitants and visitors included in the pages of this book are too numerous to mention in this index due to space limitations.

265

267